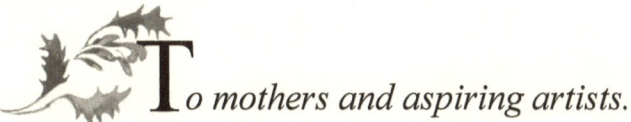

To mothers and aspiring artists.

Felicity
ART, WAR AND PEACE

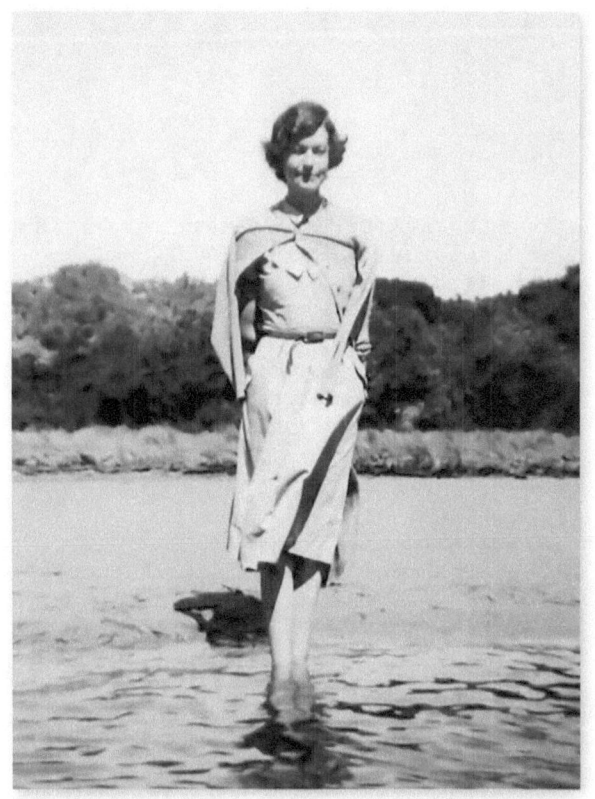

Felicity at Lake's Edge, near George, South Africa, c.1952.

PIERS R. BLACKETT
ANNAH OTIS

Copyright © 2022 by Piers R. Blackett and Annah Otis
ALL RIGHTS RESERVED
Images and text may not be reproduced in any form whatsoever without permission.

Visit our website for galleries of Felicity Blackett's art and links
for ordering e-pub and softcover versions in color.
http://www.felicityblackett.com

Editing and project coordination: *Grace Sutton*
Pre-production and design: *Claude De Backer*

On the cover: *Scottish Landscape*. Mixed media.

Contents

    Acknowledgements 1
    Introduction 3
1 Setting the Geographical and Genealogical Scene 5
2 A World at War 11
3 From the Scottish Border to the Italian Lakes 19
4 Felicity Finds Her Footing 29
5 Tying and Untying Knots 35
6 Dodging Bullets 45
7 With Death Comes New Life 53
8 The Blacketts Brave Germany 57
9 On to South Africa 67
10 Life as They Knew It 73
11 Comings and Goings in Cape Town 83
12 Homeward Bound 93
13 A Mole, A Wizard, and A Scotsman 101
14 The Waning Years 111
    Remembering Felicity 115
    Family Tree 120
    Selected Bibliography 121

Acknowledgments

In considering the best way to present my mother's art, I realized that to do her justice, I needed to place her life's work in the context of the places and turbulent times through which she lived. In order to do so, I started down a lengthy path of historical research. Then I came to realize that the narrative needed more creative flare than an author accustomed to medical and scientific writing could manage alone.

The book thus became a family project in which my grand-niece, Annah Otis, applied her talents as an English and Art History major at Georgetown University to turn academic prose into a coherent and exciting story. My half-sister Joannah Wilmerding, Felicity's oldest daughter, was an inspiration and driving force throughout the project. She collaborated to edit the manuscript and to select, annotate, and place artwork within the chapters, assisted by her daughter Felicity Wilmerding.

Above all I would like to thank Annah, for unwavering application of her writing and editing skills, her concept of effectively placing photos and paintings throughout the text and for patience in seeing it all gel together. Other family members have been drawn into the project in one way or another, especially Felicity's younger daughter and my sister, Miranda. I am grateful for all the information, advice, and encouragement they have provided.

On the production side, Madison Photo and photo restoration specialist Mary Horn have done wonders to enhance images as needed, especially the vintage photos from Felicity's early years. Working with us on design were Claude DeBacker and Grace Sutton, whose expertise and good eyes were equalled only by their patience.

Piers R. Blackett, 2022

River Arno, Florence. Mixed media.

 Introduction

Felicity Blackett (1912-2011) began pursuing a career in art when she was at school on the Italian Riviera. Her epic story is an inspiring account for those who love art and the life it represents. We, the authors, present it as a message of hope and encouragement, not only for those who are aspiring artists, but also for those who endured the same tragic twentieth century events Felicity did.

Significant historical events shaped Felicity's character and direction from an early age. Despite the setbacks posed by two world wars, she developed a unique style and embraced female independence. Her widowed mother was determined to give Felicity a positive upbringing and education regardless of where they were living. Finding a suitable school in Italy was challenging, but finding a good art teacher less so. After returning to England as a young woman, Felicity met her first husband and gave birth to a baby girl. The union lasted less than a year. She began training as a nurse when WWII broke out, and fell in love with the man who was to become her husband while he was convalescing from a wound sustained on the front lines. The couple had two children before moving to Germany on military assignment and then to South Africa. Felicity's time in South Africa was conducive to drawing and painting from live subjects. She and Rupert moved back to Britain in 1975, but separated amicably a few years later.

Felicity then lived in the Gloucestershire village of Dursley, during which time her artwork was twice accepted for exhibition at the local Royal West Academy exhibits. She became a member and frequent visitor of the nearby Slimbridge Wetland Centre because of the birdlife sketching opportunities it provided. In the 1980s, Felicity began keeping a diary to record her early years and reflect on the present ones. It was rediscovered when her house was sold and has been indispensable to her biography. Several quotes are included throughout this book to describe poignant moments and important transitions from her point of view.

The book concludes with a short chapter on Felicity's transition to old age, which serves as a sad yet enriching example of continued artistic aspiration. She died peacefully at the age of 99, by which time she had become a well-loved member of many communities throughout the world. Felicity's son and great-granddaughter worked together to catalog her remarkable life. The resulting book is a biography of a woman whose verve and empathy touched so many.

1
Setting the Geographical & Genealogical Scene

By the time Felicity was born in 1912, her hometown of Liverpool was already a thriving industrial center with a growing population and considerable ties to the global economy. What had once been a sleepy fishing village nestled along the River Mersey found itself in the midst of an international trading boom involving cotton from the United States, sugar from India, and coal from British mines.

Everything eventually found its way to Liverpool's docks where shipping companies, primarily the Cunard and White Star Lines, facilitated worldwide distribution. Massive freighters lumbered towards land around the clock as raw materials and finished products flooded in. The nearby towns of Birkenhead and Wallasey enjoyed similar prosperity after the Royal Navy and the Mercantile Marine established ship-building centers along England's northwestern coast.

English industrial success was a magnet for struggling Welsh families, famine-battered Irishmen, and Chinese sailors seeking employment on shipping lines. Thousands of migrants flooded into Liverpool in hopes of finding steady employment. Tenements soon overflowed with laborers who spent the daylight hours

Billy Smith mounted on parade as Head of the Criminal Investigation for the Liverpool Police, **1913**.

toiling away in often unsafe situations. Poor living conditions, high mortality rates, and unchecked diseases did little to staunch the flow of people. An especially robust Welsh community lent Liverpool the unofficial title, Capital of North Wales.[1]

The Graham Family Crest. "Never Forget"

Felicity's parents were among those who found their way to Liverpool by the turn of the century. William "Billy" Alfred Smith and Alice Graham married in 1908 as the first tremors of unrest began to reverberate through Europe. The young couple's resilience in the face of adversity would prove essential in the coming years.

Billy's early life was spent in Herefordshire not far from England's western border with Wales. Acres of pasture populated by horses and cattle abutted a lovely country home known as Gattertop. The Smiths successfully raised Herefords, a local breed of white-faced cattle prized for their beef as well as their ability to thrive in temperate climes.[2]

A Hereford bull named Brewster took home second prize at an agricultural fair in 1903 and subsequently sold for today's equivalent of ten thousand pounds.[3] Notices in Herefordshire newspapers indicate that the Smiths also produced a number of award-winning horses which grazed side-by-side their stockier bovine companions.

Both of Billy's parents led active social lives. His father, William John Smith, served as the president of the local Land and Labor Defense Association in addition to representing the Herefordshire Hop Growers. The latter required he represent fellow farmers before the House of Commons in London. Not to be outdone, Billy's mother hosted church events and fundraised tirelessly for a new vicarage in Monkland. She was a hardy woman who raised twelve children and lived to the age of ninety-nine. All of the little Smiths were recruited to lend a hand in their parents' charitable efforts. Billy thus spent his youth in the service of family and community; his adult years would be devoted to the same.

Cambridge University drew Billy away from the grassy midlands of Herefordshire to the well-kept quads of Pembroke College. His studies fostered an interest in public service, which led to his involvement with the University Officers' Training Corps. The Cambridge unit had been established in 1803 to prepare for an invasion against France during the Napoleonic Wars. By the late nineteenth century, it had become a vetting ground for potential recruits to the South African War.[4] Billy chose not to pursue a military career and instead joined the Royal Irish Constabulary after graduation. By the time he met Alice, the young man was already a successful detective for the Liverpool Police Department. Alice enjoyed a privileged childhood in a country manor along the Scottish border in Dumfriesshire. The sprawling Mossknowe estate included several outbuildings and a large main house punctuated by two tall groups of chimneys. As at Gattertop, cattle grazed freely in the large fields nearby.

Setting the Geographical & Genealogical Scene

The property came into the family when a University of Edinburgh-trained minister named William Graham married Margaret Irving, the sole heir of Sir David Irving's estate, in 1660. Mossknowe was inherited by a succession of eldest sons, most of whom were also named William, until reaching Alice's father in the late nineteenth century.

Sir John Gordon Graham and his older brother grew up at Mossknowe under the watchful eye of their father, yet another Sir William Graham, who served as a colonel in the military. John followed in his father's footsteps by becoming a Major General in the First Royal Dragoons. He married a similarly well-stationed lady named Susanna Elizabeth Hay Graham, the daughter of Sir Arthur Hay and Thomasina Isabella Johnstone Hay. Susanna and the couple's eight children kept Mossknowe lively during William's long absences on military deployments.

Sadly, Susanna passed away when Alice was in her early twenties. The heartbreak would have been unbearable if not for the support of an older sister named Violet and a younger brother, named Claude. The threesome remained close throughout their lives. Alice met and married Billy three years later.

---

[1] Muir, Ramsay. *A History of Liverpool.* 2nd ed. London, England: University Press of Liverpool, 1907. P. 243-268
[2] "History." *The Hereford Cattle Society.* Web.
[3] *Hereford Journal,* April 18, 1903, p. 5.
[4] Spiers, Edward. *"University Officers' Training Corps and the First World War."* COMEC Occasional paper No. 4. 2015. P. 8.

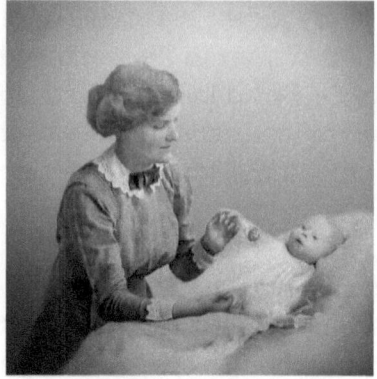

Alice with Felicity as a baby, c. 1912.

Billy and Alice sit in the sun with Felicity, 1913.
A stroll with lessons through Sefton Park, c. 1914. >

Father and daughter together during Billy's leave from the front for the last time, 1916.

2

A World at War

Times were changing, not just for Alice and William, but for Britain as a whole. Queen Victoria's death in 1901 shook the country to its core, and the economy experienced an unprecedented slump. King Edward VII reigned between 1901 and 1910 before George V succeeded to the throne alongside Queen Mary.[5]

Yet, monarchical changes failed to mend England's widening gap between the rich and the poor. Industrialization and agricultural mechanization gave Britain a financial boost, which was followed by widespread urbanization. Cramped, squalid conditions bred crime-infested cities not unlike those portrayed in Charles Dickens novels.[6] William's appointment to the head of the Investigation Department in 1912 exposed him to Liverpool's poverty-stricken masses. Alice's charity work likewise revealed how the less fortunate lived.

Britain's lacking social support systems prompted a number of early twentieth century reform movements. Prime Minister Herbert Asquith and Chancellor of the Exchequer David Lloyd George pushed ill-fated legislation through Parliament with the Labor Party's backing.[7] Workers' compensation, unions, poverty relief, and increased taxes on the wealthy came too late to stop the effects of centuries-long oppression. Production screeched to a stop when thousands of railroad workers and coal miners went on strike throughout the early nineteen hundreds. It would take two world wars and the ensuing legislative overhauls to set England's social structure back on track.[8]

National morale took another blow when the Titanic sank on April 15, 1912. The ship was originally scheduled to depart from Liverpool, but ultimately set sail from Southampton to generate more publicity. Among the 1,503 dead were community members whom Alice and William had once known.[9] Six weeks later, the couple welcomed their newborn daughter into a rapidly changing socio-political climate that would erupt into war during the summer of 1914.

Britain's nineteenth century involvement with foreign powers foreshadowed bloodier clashes to come. In 1853, the Ottoman Empire appealed to Britain and France for help against Tsar Nicholas I and his Russian army. A long-standing dispute over access to the Holy Land was beginning to erupt into violence, and the two western powers had vested interests in Middle Eastern trade routes. Their defensive tactics sparked the Crimean War, and along with the American Civil War, prompted the development of modern warfare.[10]

Increasingly friendly relations between England and France angered the German government, which retaliated by attempting to colonize French-ruled Morocco in 1905 and 1911. Tensions mounted further when Serbian terrorists assassinated Archduke Franz Ferdinand of Austria-Hungary on June 28, 1914.

Austria-Hungary declared war on Serbia shortly thereafter. Russia raced to support Serbia, while Germany and France were pulled into battle alongside Austria-Hungary.

Anglo-European ties created by the 1904 Entente Cordiale practically guaranteed that Britain would soon find itself at war as well. Winston Churchill, then First Lord of the Admiralty, reflected on the inevitability of a major clash several years later:

> *There was a strange temper in the air. Unsatisfied by material prosperity the nations turned restlessly towards strife internal and external. National passions, unduly exalted in the decline of religion, burned beneath the surface of every land with fierce, if shrouded, fires. Almost one might think the world wished to suffer. Certainly, men were everywhere eager to dare. On all sides the military preparations, precautions and counter-precautions had reached their height.*

Germany's invasion of Belgium on August 4, 1914 forced Britain into the fray. Belgium had been promised military support through the 1893 Treaty of London, and German leaders knew that Britain would have to throw in her cards when they invaded. British Foreign Secretary Sir Edward Grey ultimately advocated for war during a speech to the House of Commons; England allied with Russia and France shortly thereafter.

Efforts to enlist young men began almost immediately. The Secretary of State for War, Lord Kitchener, launched recruitment campaigns and heralded the importance of ample manpower. Such an approach was new to English military strategies. Traditionally, officers were pulled from the gentry and soldiers were hired from the working classes to form a professional army.

When General Henry Rawlinson asked London stockbrokers to raise a role-model battalion, it became clear that volunteer recruits were more plentiful than some had predicted. Sixteen hundred men joined that first so-called "Stockbrokers' Battalion" within one week. Liverpudlians followed suit by forming a battalion of fifteen hundred in just two days. The Eighteenth, Nineteenth, and Twentieth Battalions of the Liverpool King's Regiment were established in quick succession.

Such an enthusiastic reply to Lord Derby's call for a "battalion of pals" prompted other English communities to begin seeking recruits. The movement turned into a civic competition as cities strove to enlist more men than their neighbors. Nobody could have predicted how many would perish in the coming years.

Lieutenant Colonel William Smith in Liverpool, 1914. *Alice Smith as a Red Cross nurse in Liverpool, 1915.*

As a prominent police officer, William was charged with overseeing wartime operations in Sefton Park on Liverpool's Saint Anne Street. His primary responsibility was fulfilling the widely-endorsed "Derby Scheme." Recruitment began in September and concluded in early November, at which point William was appointed second-in-command of the Twentieth Battalion. His first few months as a Major were spent training in Knowsley Park and living in Tournament Hall, a medieval hunting lodge owned by Lord Derby himself.

The four Liverpool battalions soon began staging battles across the Lancashire countryside. Lord Derby's estate took a hard beating: kitchens were raided, horses were borrowed without permission, and several unlucky statues received remodeling. The fun and games came to an abrupt halt when the battalions were transferred from Knowsley Park to Belton Park Camp in Lincolnshire. Troops traveled eastward by train on April 30, 1915.

Their arrival in Grantham coincided with the arrival of four battalions from Manchester, and joint exercises fostered amiable ties between brigades. Though Alice chose to stay in Liverpool with Felicity, the people of Grantham readily welcomed soldiers and their visiting family members.

Almost exactly one year after the initial recruitment campaign, those training in Grantham were transferred to Larkhill Camp on the Salisbury Plain near Stonehenge for final preparations. Lord Derby stood in for King George V during a final Inspection of the Troops on November 3, 1915. William and the four Liverpool Battalions boarded a train for France the following day with news of a submarine scare and two Zeppelin attacks ringing in their ears. Nothing interrupted the Liverpudlian's journey to Boulogne, but the worst of the war was still ahead.

When the Germans failed to capture Paris and the battlespace shifted to trench warfare, digging furrows through Lancashire suddenly seemed worthwhile. The change in plans nonetheless caught the Liverpool

Brigade off-guard. British Generals decided to re-assign each battalion to units of the regular army, thus fostering a strong sense of unity amongst soldiers.

William faced even greater changes after the Eighteenth Manchester Battalion's Commanding Officer, Lieutenant Colonel Fraser, resigned from his post with a recurrent illness. Felicity's father stepped into Fraser's shoes two months before the Eighteenth Battalion was scheduled to fight offensively along the River Somme. A clash near the village of Suzanne in June 1915 claimed the limbs and lives of more than a hundred men. Another assault on the village of Montauban one month later left 173 dead. Other battalions to the north suffered heavier casualties, but the loss of life was a shock to everyone.

July brought another round of fire from German trenches at the Somme offensive. William and his battalion initially joined the Twenty-First Brigade in Trones Wood before retreating to Bernafray Wood in the afternoon. Five hundred men, about sixty percent of the entire battalion, succumbed to German gas attacks and bullets over the course of the day. The remaining officers regrouped in a former German dugout where the Twenty-First Brigade had set up headquarters.

Unfortunately, German troops were stationed on higher ground and quickly detected the British position. Orders were given to destroy the captured German dugout, which the British had taken over as headquarters. When German shells were fired, four officers died instantly; William suffered a fatal wound to the head. He was transferred to the Twenty-First Division Casualty Clearing Station in Corbie where he died on July 9, 1916. According to the British Military Archives, William's personal effects at the time of his death included an officers' advance book, a flask, a flashlight, a silver coin case, a whistle, a clasp knife, a wrist watch, a pocket knife, and a self-filling pen. William Knowles, a fellow wounded soldier who witnessed the Lieutenant Colonel's passing, wrote to a Smith sister in November 1916:

> *I'm afraid I can only give you a little of the information you required. I was lying in No 5 Casualty Clearing Station Corbie (Somme), when Colonel Smith was carried on a stretcher and placed in the bed opposite to me. He was unconscious at the time and remained so up to a few minutes before he died. The sister in charge told me that he was quite conscious just before the end though what he said I do not know. I saw the screen removed and the body was covered with the Union Jack. I could only ask that those standing near give a last salute before the body was carried out, for I was unable to move myself.*

War casualties were so often brutal and unsightly, excruciating to witness and even more painful to experience. It would be inaccurate to assume that William's passing was any different. Felicity had just turned four at the time, so her recollections of William were either fuzzy or gleaned from older family members. She nonetheless acquired Knowles' letter later in life and kept it pressed between the pages of a scrap book until her own death almost a century later.

William's death was equally mourned by fellow police officers and soldiers who regarded him with respect and a degree of awe. A commemoration was erected at the Church of Saint Anne across the street from his home on Brompton Avenue in Liverpool. Although the house was destroyed during World War II the memorial still stands. William's body remains in France at the Corbie Cemetery Extension along with hundreds of other soldiers who lost their lives during the Battle of the Somme.

Alice was once again thrown into deep mourning. Losing her mother and her husband within a few years of each other was a hard blow. Her wardrobe was transformed from the bright skirts of youth to the dark dresses of a widowed bride. Many years later, her dresses lightened to grey or dusty purple and a red coat entered the rotation. She firmly fixed Billy's two regimental badges worn on his uniform lapels when he was fatally wounded, to the frame of his photo which she, and later Felicity, always kept in a prominent place; a constant reminder of his sacrifice and that of many others to King and country.

---

[5] Wasson, Ellis. *A History of Modern Britain: 1714 to the Present.* 2nd ed. West Sussex, England: John Wiley & Sons, Inc, 2016. P. 208, 219.
[6] Liverpool City Council. *The Merseyside Historic Characterization Project:* Liverpool, England: National Museums Liverpool, 2009. P. 36-38.
[7] Wasson, Ellis. *A History of Modern Britain: 1714 to the Present.* P. 214-219.
[8] Ibid., 216.
[9] Lord, Walter. *A Night to Remember: The Classic Account of the Final Hours of the Titanic.* New York, NY: Griffin, 2005. Print.
[10] Wasson, Ellis. *A History of Modern Britain.* P. 176-179.

3

From the Scottish Border to the Italian Lakes

Widowhood was becoming less and less unusual for young English wives. World War I tore families apart and sent countless men to their hastily dug graves. Alice decided to flee Liverpool and its endless associations with her dead husband before the war took anyone else away. She and daughter Felicity moved to a village in northern Oxfordshire called Bloxham where an army hospital had taken over the grounds of a large country estate. In an effort to support her growing child while supporting the war effort, Alice quickly found work as a cook for convalescing soldiers. She was hired by a temperamental Italian chef who left town several months later, thus leaving Alice in charge of the army hospital kitchens. This experience gave Alice the courage and competence to establish a series of tea rooms after the war's end. These tea rooms would be social as well as financial lifelines regardless of where in the world she found herself.

When the war ended in 1918, Alice and Felicity traveled north to stay with Alice's older sister in Dumfriesshire, Scotland. Violet Graham was the first one to encourage

Susanna Hay Graham, Felicity's grand-mother.

Silhouettes of Felicity's great-grandparents Colonel William Graham and Ann Graham, b. Mair. Artist unknown, c. 1850.

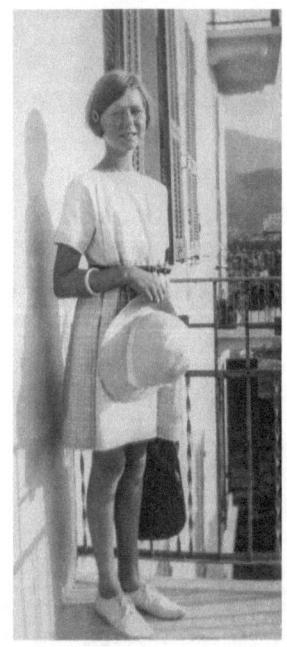

Felicty in Italy, c. 1924   *View of Alasio harbor captured by Felicity, c.* 1924.

Felicity's artistic instincts by procuring her niece simple painting materials. These would be a bright point in otherwise dark times. Sorrow had once again crept into Alice's life when her brother, Major Cecil Erskine Graham, died in battle. This tragic death was followed by another painful blow when her 'adopted' son was summoned to return home by his parents who reconsidered their agreement with Alice. In truth, the young boy was a nephew from the Smith family side whom Alice had taken in when his parents suffered a misfortune. The forced separation may have been the cause for Alice to change her last name from Scudamore-Smith, which appears on Felicity's birth certificate, to Graham-Smith which associated her more with the Graham side of the family and distanced her from the Smith side. So much loss in so little time left Alice feeling deflated and ready for a change. She ultimately decided to try her luck in Italy. The end of World War I in 1918 and Italy's friendliness with Britain made the Italian Riviera a popular destination for British citizens seeking an escape from their mother country's financial woes. This is not to say that Italy did not have troubles of her own. Mussolini united the country's fascist parties under his control in 1921, and subsequent efforts to improve the economy were largely unsuccessful. The Catholic Church's power only marginally tempered far-right policies. Units of secret police roamed the streets by 1927 and many Fascists threw their sympathy behind Germany. These developments would eventually spark an expat exodus.[11] Luckily, the Italy Alice and Felicity moved to in 1922 was not yet the dangerous Nazi-allied territory it would become.

Alice settled on Viareggio, Tuscany as an appropriate town for the time being. Felicity had been suffering from recurrent chest colds and popular science suggested that proximity to Tuscany's fragrant pine forests might be an antidote. Two of Alice's close friends, Nell and Mary Loveday, encouraged her to head south.

Felicity referred to the sisters as Aunt Mary and Aunt Nell, about whom she wrote:

> *My dear Aunt Nell had a cheerful smile ready for my mother when she heard of her loss. She lived with her sister and brother in the Elizabethan house, Arlescote, which I loved so much. Tucked under the lea at Edgehill it had a long flower border leading to a fishpond and was surrounded by tall thick yew hedges marked at the corners by gazebos.*
>
> *Within one was an oil-stove where Aunt Mary made jam; she took her cigarettes with her which she smoked in a long holder, and she had a long wooden spoon with which to stir. Aunt Nell kept bees and toward the end of my annual 3-week stay she used to dress up in the strange-looking beekeeper's clothes; and telling me to be very calm she would serenely remove the top of the hive and show me the honey inside.*

A cousin of Nell's named Lady Griselda Cheape was eager to send her own daughter, Jean, to the rejuvenating Tuscan countryside as well. Felicity elaborated:

> *Aunt Nell's cousin, Lady Griselda Cheape, who was Clementine Churchill's aunt, used to come and visit my mother on the most stormy and wildest of nights. Her black clothes must have been handed down and appeared to be made of black satin reaching to her feet, which were always muddy.*
>
> *It was probably Aunt Griselda's idea we should go to Italy. She knew of a theory then which now goes by the name of aroma therapy, and at a place in Tuscany by the sea some of the finest old pines gave out a healing scent strong enough to heal one's lungs. Jean Cheape, her daughter, would join us in Italy when we had found somewhere to live. Our expeditions to Strathtyrum, their home near St. Andrews, usually included a visit to the*

> henhouse where Lady Griselda had to kneel down to persuade the hens to show themselves to me, their anxious 10-year old visitor. She even brought her guinea-pigs out to tea with her.
>
> Italy was a place where people had always gone with health problems, so my mother was urged to go where Jean Cheape would later join us. When Jean arrived, she brought a bicycle with her from which she could not be parted, but for a female to ride one was against Italian etiquette and the children used to call after her "Pantaloni Inglesi" referring to the fashionable bloomers which she couldn't help showing as she rode down the street.

The bicycle bloomers incident points to a larger clash between Italian culture and English newcomers. Alice and Felicity were joined by hundreds of other war-scarred Brits hoping to find a fresh start on the Italian Riviera. The populations in towns like San Remo blossomed, and a thriving cultural scene emerged just in time for Felicity to soak it all up. Alice recognized an opening in the buzzing social milieu for an English tea house where one could enjoy light meals or a game of bridge. The establishment drew tea-loving Britons eager to maintain their afternoon ritual.

Felicity, however, was far more interested in art than social forays or business ventures. Alice quickly recognized her daughter's budding artistic talent and arranged for lessons with an English teacher named Barbara Nash. Barbara's two brothers, Paul and John, were gifted painters who worked as official government artists during World War I and influenced their sister's style. Felicity remembered those first lessons fondly:

> I loved Barbara Nash who gave me my first lessons in art. She was sister of the artists Paul and John Nash known

> for their paintings of the war and who later became known as artists and teachers. She took the American girls, including me, on sketching expeditions. We went to the beach where [Percy Bysshe] Shelley drowned, and climbed into an old boat thinking of his funeral pyre on the shore. We walked through the farms where they grew dark red clover as a crop and where the bullocks plowed the volcanic soil, large and pale-colored with mournful brown eyes. There was a little wooden bridge and a boat moored beside it, so I sat in it to paint the shore-line; and the eldest Arvine girl, Alice, painted me in the boat in a red dress my mother had made. My mother never sewed very well but kept the pictures for a long time.

As much as Felicity enjoyed her art lessons, school was also a necessity. She initially attended an English school in Viareggio whose kind Headmistress left a positive impression. Although Felicity soon became fluent in both French and Italian, Alice decided that the understaffed institution was doing little for her daughter's education. Felicity was consequently pulled out of school and taken on a trip to the Italian Lakes while Alice sought a better arrangement.

Among their adventures was a stay in Riva del Garda along Lake Garda on the southern edge of the Italian Alps. Felicity was quick to observe the ways in which war continued to reverberate throughout Italy:

> Riva was rather airless and stuffy and the castle resembled a prison since it had been used as one just like in Kafka's book. We used to hurry past it to the Lido where a wooden pier jutted out onto the lake, and Germans used to come and sun-bathe in pink bulging rows which disgusted the Lido manager. One day a German spoke to him rudely and so he put on his spiked climbing boots and walked down the row of German sunbathers giving them painful kicks.

> *The war had not been forgotten and the English still basked in their popularity. Having lived through the war and my father killed in action, his widow and child were welcome in Italy, so we met many British ex-patriots like ourselves.*

One's nationality was not so easily forgotten in an era of brewing political tension.

Proximity to various Italian lakes sparked Felicity's interest in the water. She delighted in swimming, drawing seascapes, and paddling along in a recently purchased canoe. Felicity was heartbroken when her mother later decided to trade the canoe for a portrait sitting. By then Felicity had recognized the futility in protesting; Alice was a strong-willed woman who firmly believed in her own opinions.

The trip to Riva del Garda afforded Alice and Felicity another chance to enjoy the water by boat. Felicity fondly recalled their ride aboard a paddle steamer that chugged past onlookers and startled wildlife. Picnics on the lake's islands with a clergyman and his family also inspired many happy memories. Felicity's love for the water never waned. In later years, she spent hours gazing across the ponds of Slimbridge Wetland Centre in Gloucestershire, England while capturing the likenesses of birds and depicting the water's reflections.

Art remained one of Felicity's foremost interests as she traveled through Italy, and Alice managed to arrange lessons for her daughter along the way. The eager young artist recalled:

> *Sketching was my favorite hobby when I had any paper and paints. Occasionally we found someone who gave lessons – once it was an Italian gentleman who taught perspective. He had boxes of all shapes and sizes which he piled one on top of the other and which I was told to try and draw.*

Though Alice encouraged Felicity's artistic inclinations, she was equally adamant about expanding her literary tastes. Local newspapers, Shakespearean plays, and a collection of books by Italian writers comprised Felicity's weekly reading list. She was particularly fond of Grazia Deledda, a female Nobel Prize winner who wrote candidly about the human condition and the surrounding natural world. Deledda's subject matter foreshadowed Felicity's interest in painting flora, fauna, and insects.

Weeks of travel through Italy delayed Felicity's formal education, although the experiences she enjoyed helped nurture a life-long passion for international exploration. As her teen years approached, this enthusiasm for discovery kept Alice busy.

---

[11] Dunnage, Jonathan. *Twentieth Century Italy: A Social History.* New York, New York: Routledge, 2014. P. 54-64.

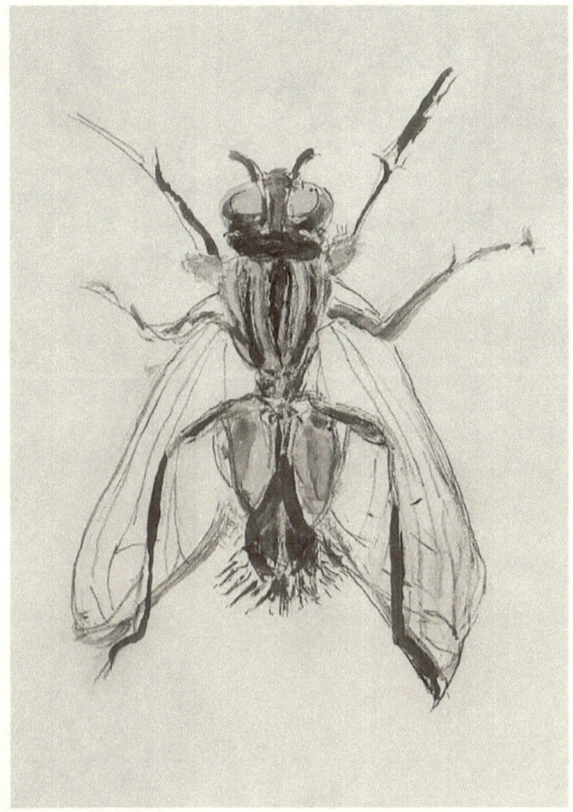

Housefly. Tempera

Felicity prepares to play tennis in the sun, **1926**.

Felicity en route to the beach, **1927**

Felicity sits in quiet contemplation, c. **1929**.

4

FELICITY FINDS HER FOOTING

The trip through Italy's Lake District gave Alice time to find a suitable school for Felicity and an appropriate locale to establish her second tea room. An English boarding school in Alassio was deemed appropriate, while Alice settled in a nearby town called Diano Marina. Felicity traversed the ten miles to her mother's cottage every weekend to continue exploring the Italian countryside. Visits to local attractions, including the seventeenth-century Sanctuary of the Madonna Della Costa in San Remo and the historic seafront square known as Piazza Bresca, gave Felicity a chance to sketch fresh landscapes and architecture. Hiking through the hills with fresh air in her lungs was a welcome change from sitting at a desk all week.

The freedom Felicity found in Italy's countryside was curtailed by a regimented academic routine. St. George's headmistress was an austere woman with high expectations and puritanical rules. It was a sharp contrast to the autonomy Felicity had enjoyed during her travels. Even the school's summer term in a mountainous Swiss village, which was intended to protect the pupils from illness, could not make up for three seasons of rigidity. This was particularly true after Felicity and a friend were sent to live in a peasant's house when the small village inn ran out of room.

A school portrait of Felicity during her time at St. George's School in Allasio, 1926.

Perhaps foreseeably, the school's stifling atmosphere sparked opposition. Felicity and several friends were summarily expelled for putting "Vaseline on the blackboard, butter in the senior's bedroom slippers, and glue on the handles of the knives and forks laid for a meal." Clearly the teachers were not amused by the serious misbehavior, though Felicity's antics were amusing in hindsight. Alice thus began searching for yet another arrangement. She finally settled on Alassio's Sacred Heart Convent. Its Catholic school offered a degree of separation from the Fascist government's emerging education policies and promised a structured experience for adventurous young women.

Felicity felt out of place as a foreigner and not a particularly religious one at that, but she nonetheless forged supportive friendships with the nuns. It is notable that Vivian Leigh, who was destined to play Scarlet O'Hara in Gone with the Wind and earn two Academy Awards for Best Actress, briefly attended Sacred Heart during Felicity's time there. The soon-to-be-star was "a different kind of girl" who was resoundingly unhappy at the convent. Felicity also wrote about a Spanish nun-turned-mystic named Josefa Menendez who purportedly received visions of Christ before dying at Sacred Heart in 1923. These two figures made Sacred Heart something of a local attraction.

Life at the convent was Spartan at best. Conversations between students were strictly limited and social time even more so. These austere conditions left a lasting impression:

> *The baths were downstairs in the cellar divided by partitions and clouds of steam. "A bath was a rare and special occasion" repeated Mother Dobson to my mother. She replied that "in England regular baths were necessary" and at last I was granted the privilege of having two every week. Compared to the chapel our dormitories were very cold, and at night we removed the newspaper from under our sailor-like suits which kept our chests warm. The sheets were icy, yet I don't remember staying awake long, but just thinking of waking at night to see the watching figure of a nun in a pool of light telling her beads or reading her devotions.*

Felicity's description is eerily similar to the ones Mass Observation diarists would record during World War II. Beginning in 1937, the British government enlisted about 500 volunteers to record daily life by answering questionnaires or writing diaries. Their war-era entries describe retreating to cellars during air raids, struggling to bathe regularly because of bomb-burst pipes, freezing at night for lack of heat or window panes, and praying that they would survive Luftwaffe attacks just one more night.[12] Forced frugality at Sacred Heart prepared Felicity for later hardships, whether she realized it at the time or not.

Felicity generally remained at school through the holidays, and Alice visited only occasionally because running the tea room was a full-time commitment. Being separated from both parents was very hard on teenage Felicity. She yearned for her mother's attention almost as much as she dreamt of her father's resurrection. It was a cruel blow when Alice missed a visiting day; Felicity retreated to her dormitory in a flurry of tears and heartache.

Most of the Sacred Heart girls' time was spent inside the convent walls with few opportunities for artistic expression or physical activity. This changed for Felicity when Alice decided that Catholic boarding school was not ideal for an adventurous fifteen-year-old. Felicity soon became the convent's only day student and took up residence at a nearby villa owned by two artists, Harold and May McCall. The couple encouraged Felicity to develop her artistic talents alongside their students-in-residence. Felicity described her new environ with fascination:

> *May and Harold had pupils from England to learn wood engraving and lettering. Harold had emphysema and kept a tube inserted into his lung. Despite this his lettering in script on parchment was unsurpassed. They had a handpress and printed May's poems and bound them Italian fashion in soft leather. May would ask me to set out our tables and chairs on the olive terraces for the pupils and they could spend happy days with olive wood blocks and tools, or going for expeditions to make sketches.*
> *They used to love theatricals and dressing up as Gilbert and Sullivan characters. May even once took me for a picnic rather than venture forth alone in the autobus, so we rattled*

> up the valley to walk over the hilltops and explore along the cobbled streets where donkeys carried oads of flowers for the market. When everyone else was working, May said I should be doing homework, but I was not allowed to take any school books out of the convent building so I wandered through the olive groves sketching on Sundays.

Ever eager to expand Felicity's horizons, Alice convinced a philosopher named Thomas Mann to tutor her daughter once a day outside of convent curriculum. Mann later won the Nobel Prize for Literature in 1929 for his book Buddenbrooks. Life outside the convent was infinitely more engaging than life within, though Felicity continued to trek over the hills for her classes. The walk between Sacred Heart and Villa Juanita offered a glimpse of Italy's economic as well as political climate. Felicity wrote of soldiers clamoring for dinner at an army base and undernourished orphans running behind the village priest. She loved to see the happy children waving after Father Don Albino. At least Villa Juanita always provided a full plate; May was not one to skimp on food despite the encroaching agricultural crisis.[13]

Alassio in the twenties was not yet taken over by wealthy Englishmen's summer residences. Villa Juanita and the largely untouched surrounding countryside gave Felicity a great degree of freedom during her last three years at Sacred Heart. Alice cast a watchful eye over Felicity's life by maintaining correspondence with Harold and May. There was very little time for her to visit while operating her seaside tea room. Felicity remembered her mother's business as a typically English establishment acquired from a family that had fallen on hard times:

> [My mother] had met a Miss Glover whose family had suddenly lost their fortune and who had run the tea-rooms down on the Corso near the sea – intended for English people who could read their papers and pour real tea out of china pots and sit on red silk-covered sofas. She loved china

and collected it in a room leading off from the main eating place. Like the tea rooms in Rome it was a meeting place for many interesting but often odd and lonely characters. It opened from October to May and an English girl always came out to help my mother as her waitress.

The tea room's success was gradually overshadowed by Italy's political deterioration. Its Fascist government was an increasingly unpredictable entity feared by England and her allies. Brits began to make their way back across Europe towards safer ground, taking their tea-drinking pastime with them. Alice decided that it would be an opportune time to return to England with then-eighteen-year-old Felicity. Their move would inspire a new set of lessons on life, love and war.

---

[12] Mass Observation, 1937-1950s. Mass Observation. http://www.massobs.org.uk/ mass-observation-1937-1950s

[13] Dunnage, Jonathan. *Twentieth Century Italy: A Social History.* New York, New York: Routledge, 2014. P. 77-79.

5

TYING AND UNTYING KNOTS

When Alice and Felicity returned to England in 1930, they settled along the River Ex in Chilly Bridge. The cottage Alice purchased included a carefully kept garden and space for Felicity's loom, on which she used to weave tweed. The finished cloth was sold to supplement the earnings from a third tea room. Mother and daughter hardly made a fortune off their handiwork, but ever-generous Alice made a point of donating to her favorite charities on a regular basis. An enlightened upbringing had taught her the importance of helping those less fortunate.

For Felicity, the demands of commercial weaving were balanced by frequent forays into the surrounding countryside. Two of the neighbor's teenaged children, Peter and Kitty, invited Felicity to ski with them in southern France on several occasions. Closer to home, horseback riding became a favorite pastime. Felicity was a member of the Dulverton Hunt by her twentieth birthday, so many weekends were spent galloping across fields after fox and hounds.

Felicity holds Misty, Alice's Pekinese, while Alice looks on, **1930**.

View of the Solway from the Stinchcomb Church. **Mixed media.**

Foxhunting could turn dangerous at a moment's notice if a horse fell or misjudged one of the massive ditches lining farmers' properties. However, it was a casual countryside ride that ultimately left Felicity out of commission on several fronts. An unruly horse thrust Felicity from the saddle onto the ground where she lay in pain with a broken right arm. The injury prevented her from taking university entrance exams, thereby preventing her from following a dream to read languages at Cambridge. University shuffled out of the picture and war emerged at the periphery. Felicity solemnly resigned herself to domestic life, at least for the time being.

Respectable young women who did not pursue further education were expected to marry. The man who won Felicity's hand was living on his family's estate in Dulverton when the couple met in 1932. Thomas Lionel Ashburner Clapton, known to friends and family as Tommy, was a recent graduate of the Royal Military College, commonly called Sandhurst, whose father had served during World War I as a navy captain. His mother, Mildred Ashburner Clapton, met Thomas Clapton Sr. on a cruise that was supposed to improve her wavering health. Instead, she fell in love. The conservative Ashburner family disapproved of Mildred marrying a seaman, but Mildred could not be swayed and she married her sweetheart despite the family's reservations. While still serving in the British Royal Navy in 1919, Captain Clapton tragically succumbed to the Spanish Flu, leaving Mildred and Tommy as adrift as Alice and Felicity after Billy's death.

Both Felicity and Tommy were energetic, independent individuals who delighted in racing along the countryside by horseback or motorcar. Tommy found himself unemployed during Britain's Great Recession, but he was determined to make the best of things. Felicity tagged along as he helped impoverished locals find another meal or a clean pair of trousers. She later remembered:

> Tommy was momentarily interested in the idea of helping the jobless in the thirties and used to work with them when they called at our Devon cottage leaving a note on the gate for the next man. I was encouraged to take out food and cups of tea before they moved on with their small gift of money. Then on one of our motor drives we stopped to feed a tramp with the packed lunch my mother had provided only to find on reaching home some silver spoons had gone with it.

In 1938, the young couple were engaged and married with Alice's blessing. Tommy was a Captain in the Durham Light Infantry at the time and soon departed with the regiment for India. Never one to pass up an adventure, Felicity joined him.

Early to mid-twentieth century India was a country on the brink of new beginnings. British governance only lasted until 1947, and inklings of self-rule were evident much earlier. Felicity and Tommy technically lived under the British Raj, but they were surrounded by the impassioned followers of Mahatma Ghandi and Jawaharlal Nehru. Mounting anti-colonial sentiment and declining British influence were early indicators of the tragic strife to come.[14]

Tommy's military responsibilities in India's volatile political climate left him incredibly busy. But even the busiest high-ranking British officers found enough free time for polo matches, exploratory jaunts, hunting expeditions, and cocktail parties. Army wives likewise enjoyed access to British India's high society happenings. Felicity, forever intent on upturning expectations, turned away from bridge and sewing circles in favor of attending the Bombay Art School. She appeared on the first day of classes to discover several shocking realities:

> Bombay Art School would have pleased Queen Victoria. No nudes but huge metaphysical studies by groups of people labelled "Lore and Death" and "Despair" etc. with all the actors fully clothed – otherwise we drew live portraits and so learned to distinguish between different tribes and casts in which each had their distinctive manner of wearing the hair, caste marks, etc.
>
> If the model failed to turn up we knew there had been a skirmish about religion – even a murder on the bus. No pupil ever made me so ashamed or awkward about my ignorance and odd appearance although I was the sole female and wearer of a white skin and spoke no word of any Eastern dialect. My first efforts were too bad to keep but I think our instructor taught us all to see, and to concentrate.

Neither seeing nor concentrating have been known to save a marriage. Bombay's tense atmosphere filtered into Tommy and Felicity's home. Their relationship had been strained by life abroad and the only mutually beneficial option was to file for divorce. Felicity was condemned to the short end of the separation stick. As a woman, blame for the marriage's dissolution fell on her shoulders. No respectable wife voluntarily left her husband's side, especially if she was pregnant with his child. Felicity was already well into her second trimester when the pair decided to separate. Neither of their families were particularly pleased with the development. Fortunately, Felicity had independence and self-confidence *in spades*, which would be indispensable in combating withering social criticism.

Tommy and Felicity's divorce was finalized shortly after their daughter, Joannah Felicity Touchet Clapton, was born. Life as a single mother was not easy. Felicity struggled to distance herself from the shame of divorce, and her conservative tight-knit community made it especially hard. Some went so far as to ignore her altogether.

Ironically, World War II gave Felicity another chance to establish herself as a virtuous young woman. She and months-old Joannah moved north to Buckinghamshire in hopes of starting over. Helen Loveday, who had encouraged Alice to live in Italy fifteen years earlier, had a family home where Felicity rented rooms. She quickly bonded with a daughter of Alice's close friend. Both Felicity and Phyl Mason, whose second husband was descended from the poet William Wordsworth, had young children. It was a great relief to be able to confide in one another over shared struggles.

Felicity as a nurse at Tusmore House during WWII, 1939.

While Felicity was settling into life as a single mother, England was launching herself into wartime productivity. Men and women answered their country's call for service for the second time since 1900, though with considerably different weapons in hand. Numerous nursing, communications, intelligence, and manufacturing units sprang into action across Britain.[15] Felicity, too, felt the pull of duty despite her many years abroad. She became determined to join the Voluntary Aid Detachment (VAD), a group of civilians who cared for wounded soldiers, as fighting intensified across the channel. Large cities like London and Bristol suddenly found themselves pulverized by German bombs, so inhabitants had little choice but to evacuate or retreat to overcrowded shelters. The rush of people made war seem very near indeed:

> *As the cities emptied, every safe place in the country became crowded with refugees. At this point my ex-husband provided a cottage and a nanny both of which I accepted, hoping to finish my VAD training and get work.*

Tommy thus remained a supportive figure despite his pressing military life. Upon completing the requisite courses, Felicity was assigned to a country estate-turned-hospital in nearby Bicester called Tusmore House. The large manor opened its doors to hundreds of air force and army casualties. Among Felicity's assignments was turning on the air raid siren, a merciless responsibility that constantly reminded her of the ongoing war.

Single life did not suit Felicity. Her first tumultuous relationship had ended in disappointment, but not discouragement, and she warmed to the idea of finding a more compatible life partner. Captain Rupert Blackett simultaneously satisfied this longing and brought the war closer to home. Coincidentally, Rupert had served in India with Tommy as a member of the Durham Light Infantry and had been named Joannah's godfather. He was a well-liked man whose military career began after he finished reading law at Lincoln College at Oxford University. He climbed the ranks from Second Lieutenant to Major over the course of his service in the Infantry.

The Blackett Family Crest, "We work in hope."

Rupert Blackett and his Labrador Mary, 1939.

Friendship became romance when Rupert began visiting Felicity during his periods of leave. As with many war-time couples, their relationship developed quickly. A late 1939 visit to the Blackett estate in Northumberland gave Felicity the chance to meet her future in-laws. Sir Hugh Blackett was a community-minded individual who served as Captain in the Northumberland Yeomanry, Justice of the Peace for Northumberland County, and High Sheriff of Northumberland, while Lady Blackett, née Helen Lowther, raised their four sons at Matfen Hall. The baronetcy was originally bestowed on Sir William Blackett by King Charles II as a reward for supporting the Royalists during England's Civil War of 1642-1651.[16]

The Matfen Hall Felicity visited in 1939 boasted an impressive art collection and an expansive property, where the Blackett brothers used to ride horses, foxhunt, and shoot birds. Two of these brothers, Douglas and Francis, both served as Majors in the cavalry. Each returned from war with tales of daring and hardship. Douglas was first arrested by the Nazis in 1940 while serving in the Africa Campaign. He was taken to Italy where he escaped from a moving train. He and his two companions waited till the German guards were occupied and rolled with the fall – a trick they had learned riding horses. Unfortunately they were seen as being too unlike Italians and were apprehended by German guards near the Swiss border and close to freedom. Recaptured, he was sent to Germany, where he survived the Brunswick concentration camp. Francis had a brush with glory when he defeated an enemy fighter in hand-to-hand combat. The third brother, George, suffered a developmental delay precipitated by a rubella virus infection that disqualified him from service. Nonetheless, his humor and kindness made him a popular figure in the Northumbria community. George succeeded his brother as the tenth baronet in his later years.[17]

In one of her letters Felicity acknowledged Rupert's strong attachment to his Northumberland roots and wistfully commented that she had never felt a similar attachment to a place. Her father-in-law continued to live at Matfen Hall until his own unfortunate demise in 1961 when the manor was subsequently leased to the Leonard Cheshire Foundation as a home for the disabled. When the Foundation's lease expired twenty five years later, twelfth baronet Sir Hugh Blackett and his wife Anna renovated Matfen to become an award-winning four-star hotel. When Hugh and Anna accepted a bid for its sale in the summer of 2020, Matfen Hall's reputation for excellence continued.

---

[14] "Situating India." *India: Emerging Power.* Washington, DC: Brookings Institution Press, 2001. P. 17-35.
[15] Wasson, Ellis. *A History of Modern Britain.* P. 301.
[16] Kirtley, Allan, Patricia Longbottom, and Martin Blackett. *A History of the Blacketts: The Story of a Remarkable North-East England Family Over Seven Centuries.* England: The Blacketts, 2013. Print.
[17] Ibid.

6
Dodging Bullets

Rupert's regiment was shipped to France in anticipation of a German attack on Normandy in early 1940. Plans quickly changed when Germany invaded Belgium, and British troops were called in to secure a natural defense line along the Dyle River. Thousands of refugees streamed westward as the soldiers marched in the opposite direction. Stories of torture and death hung in the air even as crowds gathered to wave flags and cheer on the ranks. Civilians promptly scattered when the British army finally made contact with Germany's 31st Division on May 14, 1940 near the village of La Tombe,[18] the headquarters for Rupert's platoon.

An intense few days of fighting put British units on the defensive. As German machine gun fire rained down, allied defense operation teams raced to destroy bridges and halt enemy advances. Among them was Captain Richard Annand VC, an officer and Northumbrian like Rupert, who was tasked with a grenade attack on German bridging parties. His actions and subsequent honor are known as "The Wheel-Barrow VC" in part for his rescue a severely wounded comrade who was later captured by the Germans and admitted to a Dutch hospital where he died from battle wounds. Captain Annand was nonetheless the first World War II soldier to receive the Victoria Cross for bravery. Sometime later, he recalled fighting alongside Rupert, his company commander, before both sustained injuries.[19]

The Dyle encounter shattered any illusions of invincibility. Even the Germans later referred to the incident as "Hell on the Dyle" on account of British stoicism. Unfortunately, it would take much more to rescue Europe from Hitler's clutches.[20]

Marabou Sensing Danger. **Dry point.**

On the afternoon of May 15, Rupert recognized a weak link near an area held by the Welsh Fusiliers and ventured from his post to confer with the commanding officers. Bullets and bombs continued to fall amongst the ranks, hitting some and narrowly missing others. Rupert dodged a direct hit, but was seriously wounded by falling shrapnel. The Welsh officer he had been speaking to quickly dressed the wound as German soldiers began breaking through the front lines.

Rupert was left to fend for himself as his comrades retreated. An agonizing journey on all fours brought him to a nearby chateau, where he paused to regain strength before crawling after the fleeing British army. He was eventually rescued by a soldier whose haphazard driving left both passengers and the Jeep in a ditch. Another car driven by Army Chaplain Rice soon stopped to pick them up.

A blood-soaked, nearly unconscious Rupert was driven to the field hospital where doctors and nurses scrambled to pack up ahead of the advancing Germans. Yet, Rupert's injury was deemed serious enough for a pause in the commotion. A young surgeon was tasked with incising Rupert's abdomen to find shrapnel that had entered through his back. The operation was rushed and incomplete; proper surgery would have to wait until Rupert was safely back in England.

Leaving France for England was just as perilous as remaining on the battlefields. The wounded were packed onto a coast-bound train that slowly snaked through Belgium and France amidst flying bullets. A hidden channel port allowed him to reach English shores within three days. From there, Rupert was transported to Basingstoke Hospital with a handful of wounded comrades.

The hospital originally served as a mental health institute, but it was partially evacuated to accommodate returning soldiers. Several rooms remained occupied by psychiatric patients who wandered the gardens alongside recovering soldiers. Inside, rows of men lay near death. Rupert joined them after returning from a second surgery in London. His doctor issued a dire diagnosis, and the nurses followed suit with grim predictions.

Lady Blackett visited Basingstoke Hospital shortly after Neville Chamberlain ceded his position to Winston

Churchill in May 1940. Mother and son sat side by side as Churchill's inaugural House of Commons address played over the radio.[21] Rupert was well-aware of the hardships Churchill enumerated, yet he found great strength and reassurance in the Prime Minister's words.

Despite the gloomy prognosis, Rupert was well enough to return home after six weeks. Felicity greeted her husband with a heavy heart despite her recent acquisition of a nursing certificate. Proximity to wounded soldiers and Rupert's suffering convinced Felicity that England was no longer a safe place to raise a child. By mid-1940, it was clear that any decisions regarding Joannah's well-being would have to be made quickly. England was literally falling to pieces before Felicity's eyes, and like many mothers of the time, she felt that America offered a safe haven.

The Children's Overseas Reception Board (CORB) facilitated thousands of relocations to Canada, Australia, New Zealand, South Africa and the United States. It was designed and funded by the British government to remove the next generation from enemy fire. More than two thousand children participated in the program over the course of its one-year existence.[22]

The decision to send two-year-old Joannah abroad was a difficult one, both emotionally and logistically. Hundreds of families sought transatlantic passage for their little ones, even as they recognized the possibility of never seeing them again. The children in question were similarly frightened by the prospect of leaving their homes and their families; the experience left indelible psychological scars on many. Felicity recalled her experience as a parent:

> *I began to get short of money and begged the organizers to put Joannah higher on the list. Mr. Dana gave me a sympathetic hearing and we steeled ourselves for the parting. He was as good as his word and Joannah with*

> her new 60-year-old nurse Lillian Vicary had to say good-bye and join all the other children in the ball-room at the Grosvenor Hotel and entrain for Liverpool. If I had known what the physical pain of parting was to feel like, I would have tried anything to avoid it.

The stress of sending Joannah to America was exacerbated when a German torpedo sank the Liverpool-based S.S. City of Benares on September 17, 1940. Over two hundred passengers perished, including seventy-seven children. The tragedy was a public relations nightmare for the CORB, and the organization was forced to close its doors. As a result, only four evacuee ships with child passengers left England in the fall of 1940. Joannah was among the lucky few who slipped out of Liverpool before the CORB officially shut down.[23] She was originally slated to travel on the ill-fated Benares, but ultimately found herself under the care of Nanny Vicary on the R.M.S. Samaria.

Fate and imprecise maritime technology saved Joannah for the second time in a matter of weeks as she sailed across the Atlantic. Dusk had fallen and the sky was dark when an enemy torpedo skimmed past her ship. Similar ones had already claimed dozens of lives as well as thousands of precious supplies. An ocean-churning explosion perilously rocked the Samaria from side to side as young Joannah clung to her bunk in the ship's berth. Nobody was injured, but Nanny Vicary slept with a life jacket every night thereafter. Torpedoes were hardly the only danger on board. Smallpox spread to many of the child passengers during their turbulent journey. Nonetheless, Joannah arrived largely unscathed in New York City on October 3, 1940. It was six days before her second birthday.

Although Joannah's first foster home proved ill-fitting, she was soon re-assigned to live with Florence and Arthur Whitney in rural New Jersey. The Whitneys were

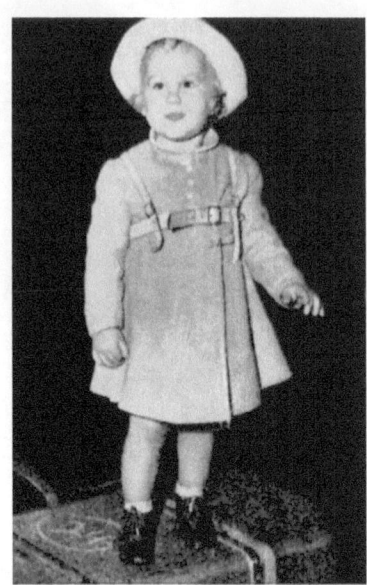

Joannah's picture appeared in a New York newspaper upon her arrival in America, **1940**.

Arthur and Florence Whitney in front of the family home in New Jersey with their Dalmatiens, **1926**.

an older, childless couple of comfortable means. Arthur was a member of the New York Stock Exchange and later served as a New Jersey State Senator, while Florence lent her support by entertaining a variety of guests and volunteering her time.[24] Joannah was a welcome distraction from the war-time politics, and she became a much-loved addition to the Whitney household. Felicity was hugely relieved to hear of her daughter's well-being and happiness.

---

[18] Rissik, David. *D.L.I. AT WAR: The History of the Durham Light Infantry 1939-1945*. Naval & Military Press, 2004. P. 12, 16, 243.
[19] "Richard Annand." *The English Light Infantry*. Web.
[20] Rissik, David. *D.L.I. AT WAR: The History of the Durham Light Infantry 1939-1945*. Naval & Military Press, 2004. P. 12, 16, 243.
[21] Lukacs, John R. *Blood, Toil, Tears and Sweat: The Dire Warning: Churchill's First Speech as Prime Minister*. New York, NY: Basic Books, 2008. Print.
[22] Welshman, John. *Churchill's Children: The Evacuee Experience in Wartime Britain*. Oxford, UK: Oxford University Press, 2010. Print.
[23] Kershaw, Roger. "Remembering the City of Benares Tragedy." *The National Archives*. September 17, 2015. Web.
[24] Johnson, Nelson. *Battleground New Jersey: Vanderbilt, Hague, and their Fight for Justice*. New Brunswick, NJ: Rutgers University Press, 2014. Print.

l-r, Alice Graham-Smith, Sir Hugh Blackett, Lady Blackett cradling Piers, Nurse Pemberton, and Felicity holding Peg the Norwich Terrier. Matfen Hall, 1941.

7
WITH DEATH COMES NEW LIFE

England's ongoing military recruitment necessitated fully-equipped training facilities and a fresh supply of seasoned officers to train new enlistees. Rupert thus made a hasty transition from home rest to troop-training on the Yorkshire Moors where Felicity and he took up residence in a rented caravan. The cramped shack-like structure was hardly the domestic utopia a young couple might imagine; it undoubtedly tested their new bond. For Felicity, living on the moors in a caravan was just one more in a long line of adventures.

War still showed no signs of abating when Felicity gave birth to her second child, Piers Rupert Blackett, in September 1941. Felicity made the most of her situation with a newborn and a tiny mobile home. She and Rupert soon relocated to a training camp in Durham sixty miles from Matfen Hall. The proximity to Rupert's family home eased some of Felicity's burdens.

The constant anxiety of war was compounded by a tragic death in 1943. January was a cold, dark month made even more so by mandatory blackouts. When Rupert's mother, Lady Blackett, ventured into Matfen's supply cellar, she slipped and fell down the steep spiral staircase. Her passing left a significant void for the Northumbria community. Lady Blackett, like Alice, had placed a premium on generosity towards others.

Thousands of miles across the ocean, Joannah was enrolled in a northern New Jersey primary school run by the Sisters of St. John the Baptist. Her foster father, Arthur Whitney, succumbed to cancer in November 1943 after a lifetime of political and philanthropic activism. Florence Whitney turned her full attention towards raising Joannah in a carefree environment in the company of children her own age. When she was not overseeing Joannah's upbringing, Florence devoted herself to volunteering for the Red Cross and the New York Hospital.

Increasingly optimistic reports from the front lines allowed Felicity and Rupert to relax into a routine as newlyweds. Rupert stayed in Durham until January 1944 when he was reassigned to advanced troop exercises at the Infantry Training Center at Catterick. Felicity delivered a baby girl named Rose Miranda Blackett in May of the same year. Miranda's birth preceded D-Day by two weeks, at which point Rupert, now a major, was called to the front lines as Britain desperately tried to defend Normandy from German forces.

Rupert arrived in France only a few days before Major Thomas Clapton died from wounds sustained during a German counter-attack near Caen. The men had remained close friends over the years, and Rupert was among the first to hear of Tommy's death. He was buried amidst thousands of other D-Day victims at the Bayeux War Cemetery in France. Joannah visited his grave almost seventy-five years later only to find with heart-broken dismay that her name was left off the headstone's list of surviving family members. She had never truly gotten the chance to know her father, and Rupert was always a kind paternal figure after Tommy's death, but the omission was still a hard blow. Ongoing communications with cemetery commissioners may remedy the mistake.

One tragedy certainly does not preclude another during war. Rupert was once again struck by rebounding shrapnel within weeks of returning to France. This second injury proved less severe than the first. He briefly joined Felicity and his two children at Cherrywood Cottage in Cookham Dean before returning to the front lines where he remained until the war's end. Felicity was left to care for her children as best she could in a time of extreme shortages.

Fire-lit, bomb-ravaged London loomed on the horizon of their small village as a constant reminder of war. Family cars were constantly parked along the streets thanks to petrol shortages. Government-issued gas masks were distributed to each family. Even the colorful masks decorated with Disney characters for children were no less ghoulish-looking than the standard adult versions. At night, Luftwaffe pilots flew overhead and occasional bursts of anti-aircraft fire crackled into the early morning hours. German bombers attacked provisions-laden ships headed toward English shores; millions put up with rationing across the country as the situation became progressively more severe. Enemy forces remained intent on starving Britain into submission. The government resorted to providing children with a foul-tasting combination of cod liver oil and rosehip concentrate to compensate for vitamin-poor diets.[25] Felicity's small brood of egg-producing chickens supplemented her family's meager rations, but not enough to save Piers and Miranda from the dreaded oil.

Rupert faced even more dismal conditions on the front lines. After crossing the Rhine River in 1944, operations included liberation of the infamous Bergen-Belsen and capturing Hamburg in the final weeks of war in 1945. Japan's surrender later that year marked the end of an unimaginably brutal conflict.[26] Joannah returned to England when the fighting ended in 1945, albeit with an open invitation to return from Florence Whitney. Felicity enrolled her two eldest children in Cookham Dean's Herries Preparatory School, which boasted an excellent art program under Miss Robinson and had recently moved to a building that had once belonged to acclaimed "Wind in the Willows" author Kenneth Grahame.[27] Felicity loved knowing that this was the same Kenneth Grahame who had frequented Alassio, Italy during her years in the same town.

Since fuel remained scarce immediately following the war, Joannah and Piers were sent to school on foot each morning. Six-year-old Joannah was charged with supervising her three-year-old brother on the long walk to and from Herries. Only once was Felicity forced to deliver Piers by car after Joannah raced ahead. The Herries School Headmistress was not amused by the situation, and she issued a strong warning against wasting petrol. Piers never again arrived at school without Joannah's supervision.

---

[25] Oddy, Derek J. "The Stop-Go Era: Restoring Food Choice in Britain After World War II." *The Rise of Obesity in Europe: A Twentieth Century Food History.* Surrey, UK: Ashgate Publishing Ltd., 2009. P. 61.
[26] Wasson, Ellis. *A History of Modern Britain.* P. 303.
*Note: Rupert was assigned to the 11th Armoured Division for the Allied invasion and advance through Europe until Victory in Europe Day (8th May, 1945) when he rejoined the Durham Light Infantry (DLI) for post-war occupation.
[27] Kuznets, Lois R. *Kenneth Grahame.* Boston, MA: Twayne Publishers, 1987. Print.

8
THE BLACKETTS BRAVE GERMANY

Japan's surrender in early September of 1946 marked the official end to war, but Rupert's responsibilities extended beyond the front lines. The Durham Light Infantry was assigned to various posts in British-occupied Germany.[28] Although families were not supposed to reunite until everything was firmly under control, Felicity was eager to rejoin her husband as soon as possible. She began making farewell rounds to various relatives in preparation for departure in spite of continued petrol shortages. The end of blackouts made everything a little easier.

Felicity first called on her beloved aunts, Agatha and Jess, with the three children in tow. Jess's husband, Dr. Bernard Wilson, was a well-respected, Vienna-trained ophthalmologist who remained on the forefront of scientific developments. Agatha and Jess were eager to acquire portraits of their great-nieces and great-nephew who had thus far only been the subjects of their mother's drawings. Piers was wrangled into a sailor suit while Joannah and Miranda posed in their best dresses. Surviving the war was cause for celebration, even if it meant watching relatives depart on new adventures.

Felicity then visited Matfen Hall to bid her in-laws farewell. Miranda remained with the housekeeper, Audrey, in Cookham Dean as Joannah and Piers journeyed with their mother to Northumberland. Rupert's father still presided over Matfen alongside his second son, George, and daughter-in-law, Euphemia. In keeping with English aristocratic tradition, the children were sequestered to the nursery under Aunt Euphemia's care. Joannah and Piers were to be seen and not heard, so they caught only passing glimpses of their mother en route to the dining room. Staying at Matfen was something like living in a fairytale castle. A full suit of armor surveyed the vaulted main hall and three stories held endless stone-walled rooms with neo-Gothic features. It was an illusion that broke all too soon.

From Matfen, Felicity made her way south to visit Alice in Kent. The short stay in Sturry gave Felicity a chance to reassure her mother that Rupert had made preparations for their arrival and would take good care of them abroad. Alice's home lay near an airfield where Felicity discreetly hired an ex-Royal Air Force pilot to fly her brood and Rupert's Golden Labrador Mary to Germany. Piers was just old enough to question flying. He had experienced the suspense of waiting out German bombing raids in which planes posed a very real threat to life. Leaving the familiar comfort of England to join his father in former enemy territory was nothing short of daunting. Many other children were similarly taken aback when their fathers returned home after years on the front lines. It was startling to have near-strangers fall back into domestic life almost as if they'd never left. And that was just the lucky ones. So many youngsters never had a chance to know male relatives at all.

As the hired plane neared its final destination, worried whispers emanated from the cockpit. It had become clear that bomb craters riddling the tarmac would obstruct landing. The group was forced to touch down in Holland, while air traffic control scrambled to find an intact runway. An airfield one hundred kilometers from their original destination turned out to be the next best option.

When the weary travelers finally stepped onto former enemy soil, Rupert came forward with a welcoming smile. The joy of reunion was tempered by the horrific reality of war-torn Germany. England was in bad shape, but Germany was much worse. Barefoot, bone-thin children wandered through flattened villages in search of food. Bread lines stretched several blocks long. Glazed eyes stared out from sunken sockets as a bruised population slowly struggled to their feet.

Silhouettes of Piers and Joannah, c. 1946. Artist: Tirsta Wolka.

Rupert was originally stationed near an army base in Hemer, but soon transferred to Celle and later moved to Minden. All three towns were occupied by Britain after the war. Hemer felt the most familiar of the three since Rupert had commandeered a large house run by two Frenchwomen there during the allied forces' advance through Germany towards Berlin. One of these women, Ruth Grohe, became Felicity's close friend. Ruth's husband owned the well-known Grohe bathroom fixture company. The Grohe clan's hospitality eased a hard transition into German life, particularly since their two children were close in age to Piers and Joannah. Rupert and Felicity remained in touch with the family long after leaving Hemer for Celle.

The winter of 1947 was the coldest on record in Germany as documented by the International Tribunal taking place in Nuremberg that year. Clouds of cold breath rose from the children's mouths as they clambered over a makeshift footbridge and into the back of an army lorry on their way to school. Piers managed to miss the truck one morning, and he spent the rest of the day meandering lost through Celle. The kindly soldier who led him home discovered that Rupert and Felicity were skiing in Switzerland. Ruth Grohe had volunteered to care for the children in their absence, but Piers had taken advantage of her kindeness.

The incident hardly discouraged Piers from unsupervised exploring. He enjoyed walking along the River Weser from the house in Minden where he could join two Polish refugees whom Rupert had released from a prison camp and hired as household help. The girls and their soldier boyfriends were friendly, but soon tired of the curious child's attention. Felicity issued Piers strict instructions to stay at home with Leshka, the thirteen-year-old nanny who later married the "Batman", a personal military orderly assigned to assist Rupert.

German wounds were slowly beginning to heal by then. Rupert was assigned to be the temporary Mayor of Minden, which among other responsibilities required writing letters of condolence to war widows. Restoring Minden's public swimming pool became one of Rupert's pet projects after experiencing just one sweltering summer. A cool dip seemed to relieve his lingering back pain, though children often stopped to stare at the scars running across his back as he rested along the River Weser where he preferred to swim.

Felicity and Rupert vacationing in the Swiss Alps during their Germany years, 1946.

Johannah, Mary the Labrador, Piers, and Miranda while in Minden, Germany, 1946.

Weekends in Minden were spent horseback riding, either for pleasure or in regimental horse shows. Felicity's soft hand and balanced seat produced slightly more successful results than Rupert's more forward approach. Even Joannah participated in children's classes with a pony named Nipper.

Horse shows and military-sponsored social events gave Rupert and Felicity the chance to connect with other high-ranking army families. War stories flowed between officers as everyone tried to come to terms with the previous few years. Felicity's diary from the time recounts a soldier's daring escape from a German prison:

> *Peter was one of the POWs who escaped. He hid in the prison rubbish and when he climbed out of the prison dustbin he had to make for a certain lamp-post where an accomplice from outside was to meet him with money and information. His unknown colleagues reneged and Peter had to find his own way by night, on foot, to the port of Danzig. There he stowed away on a steamer hidden in a coil of rope.*
>
> *After they got to sea, his cough gave him away and the skipper, a Dutchman, started to turn so that he could land him once more in occupied territory. When Peter managed to dissuade the captain, it was in Norway they finally left him and from where the British liberated him after a raid; but not before he had learnt some Norwegian, and so was useful on the next raid when he was dropped by parachute in an operation to target enemy installations and put them out of action.*

Such stories were not uncommon because many former prisoners of war were sent straight back to battle after being released from enemy hands. The psychological toll is practically unimaginable. Thousands suffered from shell shock now known as post-traumatic stress disorder.

Rupert and Felicity led an active social life, but they were also diligent about spending family time. All five Clapton-Blacketts would pile into an army-issued Volkswagen Beetle for whatever adventure the day held. The Hamburg Zoo was a popular destination as it gave Felicity the opportunity to sketch animals and the children an opportunity to admire them. Hamelin was another beloved day trip since the town featured the Pied Piper statue. Longer family vacations were usually spent at the army's lodge in the Harz Mountains where skiing and tobogganing became favorite pastimes.

Such trips were treasured occasions because Rupert was usually preoccupied with his new role as the "Mayor" of Minden and the children were busy with school. Felicity, who quickly picked up German, decided that Joannah should learn the language. While Piers and Miranda were shepherded to the English speaking school for the children of army officers, their older sister shadowed the German students chattering among themselves on their way to the local Grundschule. The crowded rows of desks and tedious coursework, mostly copying letters in script onto slate boards, left an unfavorable impression. It did not help that some classmates taunted her on the playground because her English accent and origins were associated with the enemy occupiers. War had taught some unforgettable lessons, even amongst the youngest survivors.

Supplies were slow to filter into post-war Germany. Powdered eggs and milk as well as flour and sugar remained strictly rationed. Felicity acquired a goat for fresh milk because the government's powdered alternative was tasteless at best. Felicity's art materials dwindled and her sketches were often found on random scraps of paper, a habit that persisted throughout the rest of her life. As a result, cut-out-silhouettes, the popular German scherenschnitte, are among few visual images of Joannah, Piers, and Miranda from 1947.

Wartime combat followed by two years in Germany thoroughly drained Rupert's interest in army life. The Durham Light Infantry was slated to depart for the Middle East, and he had no interest in joining them. Returning to post-war England was not an appealing option, either. Moving to Matfen Hall and joining his aging father felt like a dead end, especially since Rupert's back pain would have prevented him from enjoying country life to the fullest. Winston Churchill's general election loss in 1946 also left England's more conservative citizens rumbling with discontent. Clement Attlee and the Labor Party took charge just as a post-war economic depression set in.[29] With these deterrents in mind, Rupert turned his gaze to foreign lands. He and Felicity knew that they would eventually return to England, and in the meantime, moving to South Africa was a convenient escape from war-torn Europe.

Joannah would be moving on from Germany, too. She barely remembered her early years in America and agreed to return to Florence Whitney in Mendham. Florence assumed, and the Blacketts agreed, that there were better opportunities overseas where the economy and infrastructure were less war-shattered. Joannah flew from Amsterdam to New Jersey in May 1948. Felicity tearfully waved her eldest daughter goodbye for the second time. It was a painful parting, but Felicity saw the arrangement as a way for her daughter to attend a suitable school in a stable environment. There was no guarantee of a similar situation in South Africa. A new chapter was in store for everyone.

---

[28] Rissik, David. *D.L.I. AT WAR: The History of the Durham Light Infantry 1939-1945.* Print.
[29] Wasson, Ellis. *A History of Modern Britain.* P. 306-307.

Mother and Child. Dry point.

Donkey Cart. Dry point.

9
ON TO SOUTH AFRICA

South Africa's economic growth and farming opportunities were an appealing alternative to Europe's post-war crisis. Felicity became enchanted after listening to her uncles' stories from the Boer War. Captain William "Fergus" Graham served the King's Own Scottish Borderers for two years beginning in 1900 to help Britain claim gold-and-diamond-rich territory. Dutch Afrikaners sought control over the land too, and their aggressive guerilla warfare startled an over-confident British army. (30) Early British losses strained already under-supplied medical facilities. Captain Graham experienced his army's deficiencies when he tumbled into a ditch and sustained a kick from his horse. The attending army doctor noted a badly broken shoulder, but was unable to do anything further. A painfully bumpy journey to Wynberg, a Cape Town suburb, yielded no better news. Reconstructive shoulder surgery was fairly uncharted territory in 1902, and the doctors deemed an operation too risky.

In spite of the injury, Fergus described South Africa in romantic terms:

> *It was fascinating in the early morning on the veldt. Everything was so fresh and clean, and you could smell the vivid scent of the veldt which can be experienced nowhere else. Then to start by the moonlight and watch the day breaking, the curling mist roll away from the hollows as the sun came flashing over the tops of the mountains was a sight to remember. It was wonderful how bright the morning was. The air was so wonderfully clear and the horses were always aware of the freshness of the early hours.*

Even the poorly-staffed Wynberg Hospital had remarkable qualities:

> *There was a lawn in front with flowers and all around there were pine woods, old trees chiefly, planted by the early Dutch settlers. Behind the hospital the ground sloped to a wide valley at the foot of Table Mountain. Here the government had forests and vineyards – Constantia was the place they made the wine. Sometimes we would hire a cab and go for a drive into Cape Town. Frequently, a South-Easter blew which filled the streets with dust, shingle and small stones.*

Fergus returned to his wife Elsie at their Scottish estate, Mossknowe, two weeks before British officers signed a peace treaty in Vereeniging.[31] His untreated shoulder remained cripplingly painful for the rest of his life.

Major Claude Graham, Fergus's brother, had a much more pleasant experience in South Africa. Claude spent his military career in Egypt with the King's African Rifles, during which time he earned three Egyptian crosses and a Distinguished Service Order. He retired to South Africa where he and his wife, Ellen Graham, née Chambers, managed a prosperous citrus farm and built a rambling colonial-style family home known as Redhouse.

Together, Claude and Ellen fostered relationships with some of South Africa's eminent British figures. Claude worked with respected naturalist James Stevenson-Hamilton to preserve what is now Kruger Park.[32] Ellen spent her free time advocating for child welfare and supporting a local adoption agency. The couple also knew outspoken English protagonist Sir Percy FitzPatrick, though political connections often became tenuous as different parties struggled for power.[33]

Felicity holds Ridgy the Rhodesian Ridgeback, Piers rides Peter, Miranda holds the pony, and Rupert stands nearby at Fairsprings Farm near George, c. 1949.

The 1948 South African general election coincided with Rupert and Felicity's arrival. Field Marshal Jan Smuts ran against the Nationalist Party's Daniel Francois Malan. Dozens of signs heralding Malan's victory greeted the Blackett family as they touched down in Johannesburg in late May. As the plane circled for landing, lights all across Johannesburg sparkled to life. An awe-struck

Miranda gasped, "It's Grannie's garden!" Claude and Ellen welcomed the family with open arms. The election results unsettled many English colonists, but Claude Graham encouraged the Blacketts to maintain a positive outlook for their adopted country. He couldn't have known that the next four decades would be pockmarked by conflict.[34]

Old John. Watercolor and Conté crayon.

Rupert secured a short-term lease on a cottage with views of the surrounding mountains, so that Felicity and the children could remain near the Grahams at Redhouse, while Rupert searched for a permanent home. Those first few days in South Africa opened everyone's eyes to an entirely new way of life. Pith helmets and bush shirts replaced neatly pressed suits, while Swazi field hands filled the air with colorful folk songs. The change of scene from post-war Europe was just what Rupert and Felicity had in mind.

Rupert set off in search of a permanent home as soon as everyone was settled in their mountainside cottage. From the East Transvaal, he drove down through the vast Karoo semi-desert and on towards the southern coast. Winding dirt roads eventually brought him to George, a town three hundred miles east of Cape Town where the Dutch East India Company sourced timber in the late eighteenth century.³⁵

As George grew smaller in the rear-view mirror and Victoria Bay beckoned ahead, Rupert came across a half-completed house. It was owned by Captain Charles Southey and his wife, Deliana Southey, née Cloete, whose widowed mother lived in a large white house up the hill and had given them Fairsprings Farm as a wedding gift. Whether Captain Southey anticipated the pressure of his mother-in-law's gaze, merely grew bored with house construction, or found better accommodations elsewhere is uncertain. Regardless, Rupert's bid on the three-bedroom house and surrounding acreage was promptly accepted.

The Fairsprings house at Purchase before three bedrooms and a veranda were added as a left wing.

Felicity, Piers, and Miranda joined Rupert at Fairsprings Farm within a week of its purchase. The sale was conditional on Captain Southey's help in completing the building project. A bricklayer, a carpenter, and an elderly local gardener known as Old John were placed under Rupert's supervision.

Piers and Miranda quickly learned that Old John was an eternal spring of fascinating life stories. The entirety of South Africa's then-recent history lay nestled in the gardener's memories. His early years overlapped with numerous British-Afrikaner conflicts, and his later years were marked by the apartheid movement. In between, he worked for President Paul Kruger and saw men die in the Boer War. The stories Old John told Piers and Miranda remained with them for decades, perhaps because the South Africa they experienced as children was just as politically unstable as the one Old John remembered from his youth.

---

[30] Meredith, Martin. *Diamonds, Gold, and War: The British, the Boers, and the Making of South Africa.* New York, NY: PublicAffairs, 2008. Print.
[31] Meredith, Martin. *Diamonds, Gold, and War.*
[32] "Kruger National Park." *South African National Parks.* Web.
[33] Wessels, Andries. "An Irish Gentleman in Africa: *The Ambiguous Political and Cultural Identity of Sir Percy FitzPatrick.*" English in Africa 31.1 (2004): 5-22. Print.
[34] Waddy, Nicholas L. "The Fork in the Road? British Reactions to the Election of an Apartheid Government in South Africa, May 1948." *Historia 55.1* (2010). Web.
[35] "George." *South African History Online.* March 2011. Web.

10
LIFE AS THEY KNEW IT

Fairsprings Farm and its new inhabitants remained largely divorced from South Africa's turmoil over the next ten years, in part because the land lay seven miles away from the nearest town and also because political change was a slow-moving beast. Life in the bush was a refreshing change from the industrialized bustle of England and Germany. Water was pumped from a nearby spring, and a storage tank stood at the ready to collect seasonal rainfall. Electricity was nonexistent, so 1930s kerosene lamps lit the house. Bright white flames sometimes reached up to scorch books resting on the shelf above.

Larger fires stoked by wind from mountains to the north occasionally set the bush ablaze. There were three that erupted at Fairsprings during Felicity's time there with the most horrific taking more than twenty-four hours to extinguish. Bucket after bucket of water had to be pumped from the farm's spring before frantic neighbors were able to bring the blaze under control. Fires were both destructive and regenerative for Fairsprings in that the charred detritus acted as fertilizer by returning nutrients to the soil.

Felicity at Lake's Edge.

Piers, Miranda, and Felicity at Victoria Bay, 1950.

Miranda, Piers, and Johannah at Fairsprings Farm, c. 1949.

Many of the Blackett's neighbors were Afrikaners, but a thriving English population in and around George made for a lively social life. Families hosted regular barbeque picnics known in Afrikaans as 'braaivleis.' Afternoon tea was an English custom well established in South Africa and Felicity often asked the neighboring families to share a 'cuppa' at Fairsprings. On the other hand, Felicity also invited friends living as far away as Cape Town for extended visits. Among these were the children of Brigadier Eustace and Margaret Arderne, who Rupert and Felicity had known during and before the war. Hilary, now Butler, reminisces about their visit:

> Our mother had gone to England for a year to look for a cure for her rheumatoid arthritis, and Felicity suggested that we two, aged 11 and 9, should spend a week or two with them soon after her departure. We enjoyed our time on the farm, particularly riding their ponies, musical evenings with the neighbours, excursions to the beach and gardening projects with Felicity. I had to spend some time posing for a watercolour, her gift to our mother that still graces our bedroom in Canada.
>
> When the Blacketts moved to a home in Plumstead, considerably closer to our farm in Constantia, Felicity often visited my mother who was very crippled. They had much in common, particularly their love of art. Felicity was slim and attractive, with a very quiet voice; I never heard her raise her voice in anger or frustration, a light deprecating smile was all she seemed to allow herself, in company anyway. Her real love was painting at which she was very talented; we had several of her oils in our home.

Rupert's idea of socializing was venturing fifty miles north for shooting trips with other retired British officers and their labrador retrievers. Local wheat farmers encouraged sportsmen to contain the avian threats to crop survival, such as partridges and pheasants. Later in life, Rupert gave up shooting in favor of preserving wildlife alongside his wife. Observing antelope and other wildlife during shooting trips had given him a sense of the great beauty South Africa held. Felicity's free time was usually spent sketching or painting. Oils and watercolors were her main mediums, but etching became an exciting new frontier after she met a local artist named Gertrude Eibushitz. The two women became fast friends, and Gertrude guided Felicity through the steps of using an etching needle to draw through a waxy ground, thus revealing select areas of the copper plate beneath. This technical process required a ventilation system to diffuse fumes when nitric acid was applied to the plate to eat away the exposed metal.

During this time, Felicity sharpened her eye for detail and refined her drawing abilities. Twenty years later, these skills would become essential for her wildlife drawings, some of which she also printed. Without a proper studio and ventilation system, Felicity turned to drypoint on zinc plates. The softer surface allowed her to draw directly on a plate with a steel pointed needle, with the option to rub out images and draw others in their place.

A collection of canvases, easels, charcoals, pastels, etching tools, copper plates, watercolors, oil paints, and brushes quickly accumulated at Fairsprings. Felicity routinely packed up her materials in a sturdy wooden box for family picnics at Victoria Bay or along Kaaimans River. Another favorite pastime was to search the mountain caves for San rock paintings, three thousand-year-old sketches of wild animals typically discovered further north in the Cederberg Mountains and only rarely in the nearby Outeniqua Mountains. Their creators, ancestral San tribesmen or "Bushmen," drew inspiration from the land around them in much the same way Felicity did. She loved studying the rich natural pigments of colorful South African culture.[36]

Fruit Pickers. Dry point.

Ballots Bay also became a favorite spot for its historic intrigue. According to local lore, a **1788** shipwreck lodged the captain's treasure chest onto a rocky reef that can be seen at low tide from the beach.[37] While Felicity worked away at her sketches or pondered the Ballots Bay mystery, Rupert and the children took advantage of South Africa's warm weather. A rowing boat fitted perfectly on top of the family Ford. Fair-skinned Piers suffered many sunburns in the days before sunscreen as he romped around the countryside or laid on the beach. At night, he was slathered with egg whites to soothe the burns. Felicity later wrote:

> *Piers and Miranda were still small, and we went to picnic by a lagoon near the Indian Ocean. We went at least once a week for these picnics, sometimes taking a tiny dingy on the roof of the car into which we all four climbed and giving it*

a push glided soundlessly over the glossy surface of a river or lagoon, usually with Rupert rowing.

I always remember one such picnic. I had my paints and after lunch I wandered into the tall rushes carrying them in case there was inspiration lurking under the hot sun. I soon came into a clearing where someone had built a hut of wattle and mud, thatched nicely with rushes, and seated on its doorstep was one of those deeply lined Dutch Afrikaner women. Her skin looked like a puzzle put together very loosely and her light eyes peered at me under a homemade sunbonnet called a Kappie. In pure Dutch, she greeted me. Her pets looked nervously in my direction – a cat, a dog, a cock and some hens with a pigeon and a goat were all I could see. Her great contentment flowed out round them and we all settled down quickly while I started her portrait.

It took three sittings, and I persuaded the family to bring me back to the same place on future picnics till I was finished; but her self-contained happiness at the first sitting made an impression on me for life. She had grown enough maize for them all to eat. I was later told she had never been to a doctor and that her husband had died. It seemed that no one ever came to disturb her peace.

Afrikaners like the woman Felicity painted maintained traditional lifestyles guided by the Dutch Reformed Church. Their conservative political views, embodied by the Nationalist Party, tended to favor racial segregation and the continued dominance of white settlers. By the late 1940s, enlightened Englishmen sided with Field Marshal Smuts in support of integration. Many saw the Afrikaners as stubborn radicals unwilling to embrace outsiders. The group's earlier practice to arrange their wagons in large defensive circles called "lagers" had established this reputation many years ago.[38]

Both Rupert and Felicity were unruffled by Afrikaner politics. To them, it was far more important to foster good relationships than fuel animosity. Piers spent a week with a local Afrikaner family as part of his parents' efforts to ease cultural differences. He later recalled spending Sunday in a beautifully built Dutch Reformed Church whose pastor delivered an expressive sermon in Afrikaans. Since Piers was unfamiliar with the language, his host family's seven-year-old daughter gave him a sharp poke every time they needed to stand.

Piers' own family took a more relaxed approach to religion. World War II had diminished Rupert and Felicity's faith in the English Church, so it was unusual for them to attend services aside from those on Easter and Christmas. Bishop Gwyer once asked the Blackett children what Santa Claus had given them. Miranda enthusiastically responded, "A loaf of bread and a lump of coal!" The clergyman's wide smile was replaced by a look of surprise. Rupert and Felicity had creatively substituted the English gift-giving Father Christmas with a Scottish tradition known as First Footing, in which bread is distributed as a token of kindness and coal as a symbol of warmth.

Less important holidays and weekends were often spent on horseback. Miranda had Beauty, Piers was paired with Peter, Felicity rode a grey mare named Clementine, and Rupert owned another grey called Roy. Joannah borrowed Clementine when she visited from America. On hot days, the children rode bareback through the ocean waves as family dogs bounded in and out of the surf. Joannah briefly considered remaining in South Africa with her family. The separation from her mother and half-siblings was painful despite Florence Whitney's diligent care. She visited a local convent school to see if it would be a good fit, but the stringent religious curriculum held little appeal. As much as Joannah enjoyed spending time in South Africa, her visits were always capped by a return to New Jersey.

Alice joined Rupert and Felicity in South Africa two years after their move from Germany. Although an additional bedroom was constructed for the occasion, she ultimately settled in a nearby stone cottage where local Englishwomen gathered to play bridge or enjoy the warmth of Scottish hospitality. Piers frequently rode his pony up the road for visits. Alice delighted in lecturing her eight-year-old grandson on the virtues of a career in forestry. The child longed to be studying tortoises, wildflowers, coins, stamps, and war medals up the hill with a retired post office official named Bertram Cairncross. He nonetheless endured Alice's lectures politely and came to remember her fondly. Several years later, she moved to Southern Rhodesia, present day Zimbabwe, as a governess before returning to England where she worked as a cook until age seventy-three. A lifetime of loss and hardship had taught her to value a strong work ethic, both as a means of distracting herself from the pain and as a path to independence. She passed away from a stroke in 1953. Felicity was heartbroken by her mother's death, so Rupert travelled alone to make the burial arrangements and attend the funeral, giving him the opportunity to visit family in Northumberland.

Life moved on after death, as it had so many times before. Piers and Miranda were enrolled in a one-room schoolhouse called St. Mark's School. It soon became clear that the Headmaster's relaxed approach bred chaos, and Felicity began teaching art lessons to instill more focus in the pupils. Alice started tutoring her grandchildren to make up for the school's shortcomings. As soon as Piers turned nine, he was packed up and sent to boarding school outside of Cape Town alongside two other boys from neighboring towns. An overnight train ride brought them to the front door of a popular preparatory school where British expatriates' sons congregated to receive a rigorous education. Being so far from home was challenging, but the curriculum undoubtedly positioned Piers for later success at the Diocesan College, the University of Cape Town, and medical school.

Thousands of miles across the Atlantic Ocean, Joannah graduated from Far Hills Country Day School and began tenth grade at the Masters School in Dobbs Ferry, New York. The girls' boarding school was well-regarded for its high college matriculation rate and emphasis on Christian ethics. Joannah's memory of Masters is not entirely rosy; she bridled at the rigidity of boarding school like her mother had twenty years earlier. Regardless, she graduated in 1956 with plans to attend Sarah Lawrence College later that year.

South Africa of the 1950s was a politically and culturally diverse country in the midst of self-discovery. The Blacketts nonetheless led a peaceful life at Fairsprings Farm alongside Afrikaners, foreign farm hands, and fellow Englishmen.

---

[36] "Africa's Rock Art" Trust for African Rock Art. https://africanrockart.org/rock-art-gallery/south-africa/.
[37] Green, Lawrence G. *South African Beachcomber.* Cape Town, ZA: Timmins, 1964. P. 64.
[38] Meredith, Martin. *Diamonds, Gold, and War.* Print.

Giraffes. Pen, ink and watercolor.

11

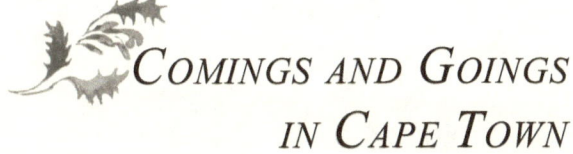

COMINGS AND GOINGS IN CAPE TOWN

South Africa's strained political climate became an immediate concern for Rupert and Felicity when they moved to a Cape Town suburb in 1958. Mornings were devoted to pouring over articles in the Cape Argus and the Cape Times. Evenings were spent huddled around a radio listening to local stations. It seemed as if the entire country was sitting on the edge of its seat. Unfortunately, access did not guarantee accuracy. The Nationalist Afrikaner government rarely allowed reporters to publish both sides of a story. Untangling fact from fiction was an endlessly frustrating chore.

In reality, Afrikaners were still smarting from the Boer War. Between 1900 and 1902, British Field Marshal Herbert Kitchener ordered his men to destroy thousands of Afrikaner properties and throw families into prison camps with poor conditions.[39] British officers attempted to right their wrongs with a lenient peace treaty at the war's end. Afrikaners were thus exempt from land taxes, granted self-government over two states, and gifted three million pounds in reparations.[40]

Miranda looks across the Outeniqua Mountains, c. 1960.

Major Claude Graham with Piers and Miranda in the Transvaal, c. 1956.

Yet, the treaty failed to extinguish the Afrikaners' political energy. It only took a few years for their Nationalist Party to set its sights on controlling South Africa in its entirety. British expatriates were horror-struck when the Nationalist Party came into power during the 1948 election and began pushing for expanded racial segregation. Black South Africans were not allowed to vote, nor were they allowed to use the same public facilities as whites.[41] Progressive English politicians vehemently protested such separation, but their cries fell on deaf ears. The African National Congress, which was organized by black activists in 1912, was forced underground in 1960. It re-emerged as the party in power after Nelson Mandela's historical release from prison in 1990 and his subsequent election as President in 1994.[42]

Prior to 1994, nothing was immune from Afrikaner influence, including the Blackett family's equestrian pursuits. Rupert had become instrumental in organizing community gymkhanas almost as soon as the family arrived in George in 1948. Riders followed a path marked by white flour through the countryside over Rupert's homemade jumps and various natural obstacles. The inaugural event proved immensely popular, but the second year was foiled by an Afrikaner politician.

Rupert and Piers were in the midst of setting up the course when staunch Nationalist Pieter Willem Botha, then a local politician, burst into their midst with a flurry of accusatory questions. Botha's internment at a British concentration camp during the Boer War bred his hatred for Englishmen and stoked his fiery temper. The aptly-named "Great Crocodile" clamped down on Rupert's gymkhana, cancelling it for no other reason than its association with an Englishman. After serving as a Member of Parliament for the town of George, he became a controversial President of South Africa in 1984, a decade before the end of apartheid.[43]

Rupert and Felicity's arrival in Cape Town coincided with the Sharpeville Massacre of March 1960 outside Johannesburg. The Pan Africanist Congress had organized a series of peaceful protests against the Pass Laws, which required black Africans to steer clear of "white-only" areas and carry pass books with their biographical information. When some of the twenty thousand protestors in Sharpeville began hurling rocks at armored vehicles, policemen began shooting into the crowd. Sixty-nine were killed and many more sustained injuries. A special United Nations committee was formed to implement sanctions, and world leaders publicly ridiculed the Nationalists.[44]

Many British South Africans had hoped for foreign intervention before tensions rose too high, but British Prime Minister Harold Macmillan dispelled these hopes with his visit to Cape Town in February 1960.[45] "The Wind of Change" speech he delivered to Parliament was named after two key lines therein:

> *The wind of change is blowing through this continent, and whether we like it or not, this growth of national consciousness is a political fact. We must all accept it as a fact, and our national policies must take account of it.*[46]

Nationalist Afrikaners interpreted Macmillan's speech as an assault on their single-minded politics, while British Members of Parliament believed the speech was intended to curb colonial expansion.[47] A less famous excerpt alludes to Macmillan's desire to appease his diverse audience:

> *Well, you understand this better than anyone, you are sprung from Europe, the home of nationalism, here in Africa you have yourselves created a free nation, a new nation. Indeed, in the history of our times yours will be recorded as the first of the African nationalists. This tide of national consciousness which is now rising in Africa, is*

a fact, for which both you and we, and the other nations of the western world are ultimately responsible.

For its causes are to be found in the achievements of western civilization, in the pushing forwards of the frontiers of knowledge, the applying of science to the service of human needs, in the expanding of food production, in the speeding and multiplying of the means of communication, and perhaps above all and more than anything else in the spread of education.

As I have said, the growth of national consciousness in Africa is a political fact, and we must accept it as such. That means, I would judge, that we've got to come to terms with it. I sincerely believe that if we cannot do so we may imperil the precarious balance between the East and West on which the peace of the world depends.[48]

Outside the political battlefield, life went on as usual. Rupert and Felicity's move to Cape Town was informed by a desire to expand their social circle, engage with the city's rich cultural scene, and live closer to their boarding school-bound children. Felicity expanded her artistic focus to painting murals and furniture decoration. Among her commissions were numerous pieces of furniture for local decorators and a mural at a fashionable club as well as one in her own dining room. The furniture decoration process was a labor-intensive job requiring Felicity to soften rabbit skin glue, add calcium carbonate, heat the combination, and brush six to eight layers of this gesso mixture onto a wooden surface. Rupert encouraged his wife to pursue the commissions, partly because they were profitable and partly because he recognized her talent for the work. Meanwhile, Rupert drew on his experiences at Fairsprings Farm to start a successful hydroponic carnation-growing business. He also spent long hours judging horse races at the Kenilworth Racecourse on the weekends.

Rupert and Felicity's fifteen years in Cape Town overlapped with significant events for Joannah, Piers, and Miranda. Florence Whitney passed away three months before Joannah's graduation from Sarah Lawrence College in 1960. Felicity mourned Florence's passing as much as her daughter did. The two women had exchanged hundreds of letters and found much more in common than a shared child. When Joannah gave her mother a pair of Florence's glasses several decades later, Felicity wistfully wrote that they were "a wonderful reminder of her and all her warmth and understanding and kindness, although she never allowed us to be mother and child."

Felicity and Piers hold Joannah's eldest daughter Felicity wearing Rupert's christening dress as he looks on, Cape Town, 1967.

Joannah went on to attend New York University's graduate School of Fine Arts at night while teaching at the Brearley School during the day and working on Greek archeological sites during the summers. She met and married a Yale graduate turned Wall Street executive named Harold Wilmerding in 1963. The couple raised five children in the New Jersey house where Florence Whitney had raised Joannah.

Piers began his university career just as Joannah was finishing hers. His determination to become a doctor from age ten onwards seemed to please Felicity. She encouraged all of her children to follow their passions, but she worried about Piers' studious nature and urged him to "lighten up" on more than one occasion. He graduated from the University of Cape Town in 1967 before interning at Groote Schuur Hospital famous for the world's first heart transplant performed by the South African doctor Christiaan Barnard. By coincidence, Piers received his degree at the 1968 graduation ceremony at which an honorary doctorate was bestowed on Doctor Barnard for his pioneering work in heart surgery. Piers' move to Durban for specialty training in pediatrics and endocrinology at the King Edward VIII Hospital, the University of Natal's teaching hospital, coincided with a strike led by Indian and black doctors protesting discriminatory work conditions. When Dr. Barnard threatened to relocate his transplant team unless the government made peace with protestors, their demands were partially met. Piers' subsequent six months at King Edward were disrupted by continual government suppression and broken promises, which eventually caused him to resign and leave South Africa. He later finished pediatric endocrinology training in Canada and the United States before accepting a faculty position at the University of Oklahoma Health Sciences Center in 1975.

Miranda attended a convent-affiliated school in George after Piers left for boarding school. She transitioned to the Herschel Girls' School in Cape Town when Rupert and Felicity moved to a Cape Town suburb. During her last year at the Barkly House Training College, the social upheaval was more intense. Although particularly so in the more densely populated northern provinces, Cape Town students on university and medical school campuses became courageous critics and activists against the nationalist government, sometimes to their cost, and some had been school friends and associates of both Miranda and Piers. As Miranda became more involved, Rupert and Felicity became increasingly concerned for their daughter's safety.

Everyone was relieved with Miranda's change of careers when she moved to London. There she enrolled in secretarial courses at Pitman's College and landed a job at Faber & Faber Publishing. Miranda met and married a Cambridge University-educated advertising executive named Merlin Pearson-Rogers in 1975. The couple had a son named Jack, but separated soon afterward. Felicity knew all too well how hard it could be to raise a child after divorce, and she was an active participant in Jack's upbringing.

Early in the 1960s before the family became entrenched in their careers or dispersed across the world, they united to board a cruise ship sailing from Cape Town to Durban. Memories came flooding back as the boat passed Fairsprings Farm and Victoria Bay where they had once ridden their ponies into the sea. A cheerful red car was hired in Durban to make the trek north towards Swaziland and the Hluhluwe game reserve. Xhosa families waved cheerfully in front of their small single room rondavels with straw roofs resembling hats as the family drove through the countryside.

Within the protection of the reserve, giraffes and an occasional rare white rhinoceros filtered across the landscape as Felicity sketched in preparation for full-fledged paintings at home. At the end of the week, everyone tumbled back into the little red car for a visit to Claude and Ellen Graham at Redhouse before the flight from Johannesburg back to Cape Town. It was a nostalgic trip that reminded Felicity of just how far she had come since arriving in South Africa a decade before.

Political tensions continued to rise after the South African Constitution Act of 1961 transferred power from Queen Elizabeth II to a National Parliament. Rupert warily watched the changes; his traditional Northumberland upbringing had conditioned him to enjoy a colonial lifestyle with proper British etiquette and recreational sports. Felicity embraced a more liberal mindset grounded in empathy for those suffering social ills. Both bravely withstood the violence engulfing Cape Town, which would simmer well after Nelson Mandela's 1994 election to presidency.[49]

Rupert and Felicity began to plan for another move shortly after Miranda left the nest. Felicity designed a new home with a garden looking towards Table Mountain, while Rupert sourced materials from traditional buildings replaced by new construction. Clara House mimicked the Dutch architectural style with a gabled front and long windows flanked by heavy wooden shutters to keep out the hot summer sunlight. It sat in a former vineyard of the fashionable Constantia neighborhood.

Despite Clara House's beauty and ideal location, Rupert and Felicity had always considered England home. The siren call to move back grew louder as South Africa's political violence escalated.

---

[39] Laws, David. *Who Killed Kitchener? The Life and Death of Britain's Most Famous War Minister.* London, UK: Biteback Publishing, 2020. Print.
[40] Davidson, W. E. *Peace Treaty of Vereeniging.* Transcript. Government of South African Republic and the British Government, 1902. Web.
[41] Thompson, Leonard. *A History of South Africa.* 3rd ed. New Haven, CT: Yale University Press, 2001. P. 142-145.
[42] Limb, Peter. *African National Congress.* Lynne Rienner Publishers, Inc., 2011. Credo Reference. Web.
[43] Thompson, Leonard. *A History of South Africa.* P. 224-225, 274.

[44] *Sharpeville Massacre.* Eds. K. Johnson and S. Jacobs. Boulder, CO: Lynne Rienner Publishers, Inc., 2011. *Credo Reference.* Web.
[45] Myers, Frank. "Harold Macmillan's 'Winds of Change' Speech: A Case Study in the Rhetoric of Policy Change." *Rhetoric and Public Affairs* 3.4 (2000): 556.
[46] MacMillan, Harold. *The Wind of Change.* Transcript. South African Parliament, Cape Town. Print.
[47] Myers, Frank. "Harold Macmillan's 'Winds of Change' Speech," 567-568.
[48] MacMillan, Harold. *The Wind of Change.*
[49] Thompson, Leonard. *A History of South Africa.* P. 241-265.

12

Homeward Bound

Rupert and Felicity followed their boxes of belongings north to Scotland in 1972. Almost twenty-five years had elapsed since Felicity first left Dover's chalk cliffs for Germany. They returned to the northern hills of Dumfriesshire, sixty miles from Matfen Hall. Rupert began a successful fish-farming venture. Felicity took to painting watercolor landscapes inspired by the surrounding countryside. Weekends remained dedicated to outdoor and social events as they had been in Germany and South Africa.

Rupert and Felicity had only just settled in Dumfriesshire when Miranda was hospitalized due to severe childbirth complications. Within days, they moved into a flat near the Frenchay Hospital to help their daughter through hard times. Frenchay had evolved from a small Quaker village on the banks of the River Frome into a fairly bustling town well-known for high-level cricket matches and a well-equipped hospital built during WWII.[50] Felicity quickly acclimated to the new community by teaching art classes at a rehabilitation center and providing in-home nursing

Felicity and Jack on a stone fence near Hexham, 1983.

Rupert at the Errington farm near Hexham, Northumberland, 1985.

services to the elderly. Her deep sense of empathy and readily available ear were endearing to lonely residents.

Rupert found it harder to adjust to life in Frenchay; his passion for sporting life predisposed him to less urban surrounds. Within a few months he accepted a farm management position near the northern town of Hexham. The job necessitated another move, but this time, Felicity declined to accompany him. Each remained devoted to the other as they started life apart. Rupert spent time with Felicity at least four times per year; she returned the favor with frequent phone calls and occasional visits.

Living in Hexham as a sheep farmer brought Rupert closer to the simple Northumberland life he had enjoyed as a child. His two surviving brothers, Francis and George, lived near enough for all three to regale tales of bygone years. In addition to sheep farming, Rupert was actively involved in training the Tyndale Hunt foxhounds. The annually-awarded Rupert Blackett Trophy for best-reared hounds memorializes his gift with animals. Chronic back pain from his World War II wounds did little to slow him down as a farmer, foxhunter, and country gentleman.

Following Miranda's recovery, Felicity moved into an ideal home in Dursley where she could reconnect with cousins living close by in the Cotswolds. The village Felicity settled in had been inhabited since the Iron Age. A nearby hill fort dates from 300 B.C.E. and Neolithic long barrows cut through the landscape. Dursley initially made a name for itself as a prominent eighteenth-century trading center and later transformed into a thriving manufacturing town.[51]

Felicity became interested in a prominent local landowner of the thirteenth century while researching her family history. She wrote, "Hugh de Audley, my possible ancestor, was Lord of the Manor, but often absent from Rangeworthy Court, his hunting lodge." The cottage Felicity lived in, which featured Georgian-era ceiling beams and three-foot-thick walls, belonged to Lord de Audley's estate ranger.

It did not take long for Felicity to fill her new garden with a veritable menagerie of animals wherein her ducks reigned supreme. They were fed chopped fish heads from the local butcher and allowed to waddle across the neatly trimmed grass. Intruding badgers were the lucky recipients of fallen apples or recently unearthed Jerusalem artichokes. Felicity also grew medicinal plants; comfrey and camomile benefited her animals and helped soothe digestive troubles. A plot of roses was the only area where animals were unwelcome. Among the pink and white blooms was a sole yellow rose that Felicity had planted in memory of her grandson Hal Wilmerding, who died in 1995 from an unsuspected heart disease. It was later diagnosed to be Arrhymogenic Right Ventricular Dysplasia (ARVD/C).

Despite having foxhunted in her youth, Felicity grew fond of a lone fox living in a nearby graveyard. He seemed to wait for her and to want to assure her that he knew her garden was off-bounds. The compassion Felicity felt for all creations large and small is palpable in the following sample of her writing:

> *A storm was raging, and the old duck found it difficult as ever to walk with the great weight of her body. Her bad eye seemed better and she ate some breakfast quite cheerfully. I will say, however, she has not been able to walk around with the others and I had been watching to see if she was in pain. As soon as I paused in front of her, she would try to talk. I heard quite intelligent sounds, but only interpreted them roughly to mean she could no longer carry the great gooselike body, so she*

let me pick her up every evening and carry her back to the run.

The last time I saw her this morning was in the run with the door open, but no fox could have had the strength to make off with her without leaving any trace of the tiniest feather. By tea-time she had vanished and, searching the garden, my heart sank and I sensed that I had said goodbye earlier in the day forever!

Then I discovered that she had climbed into the rabbit hutch there to die peacefully. The peaceful and mysterious ending saved me the sadness of taking her somewhere to be put down, but no stranger than the time when Bun climbed behind me and removed a rose thorn from my head.

Taking care of the property was a big chore for an aging, albeit very active, woman. Rupert's quarterly visits were often filled with small housekeeping or landscaping duties. Felicity recalled:

The whole garden is full of branches and trimmings. Everything grows there encouraged by the deep rich soil and I am overwhelmed by heaps which I have not the skill to deal with. Evergreen branches are piled around the car ready for me to dispose of on Monday. The man next door has a controlled bonfire which steadily smolders on most days. It is not enough to make compost. There are heaps everywhere of things that don't rot. I think of the fires in Africa that sprung up and blazed so easily getting out of control altogether. When Rupert lit one to clear some bush it burned for weeks so that he had to sleep beside it, and another which singed our back door and made sleep impossible.

A 1987 family Christmas gathering was similarly productive:

My husband and son were here for Christmas so it all seemed like the old days with Miranda and the new

> *addition to our family, dear Jack. They did so much to help. Piers cleaned out the car and they washed up in the evening when I was tired. He ran three miles before breakfast and met friends from South African days who had left the Cape with 3 children to educate. Rupert worked at caning a chair for Ferney Hill. He seemed fit and climbed the apple tree but the ladder slipped and he was only saved by falling onto the wire-netting roof of the duck's run. It gave way but the cabbages below further broke his fall, so he was alright. He slept last night in M's cottage. Piers left for Heathrow the same day as he caught the train to Newcastle.*

Such reunions were highlights, but life was hardly lackluster for Felicity when family members dispersed. She frequently ventured down to the village where business owners readily conversed. Even as chain stores like Safeway and Sainsbury began trickling into Dursley, Felicity remained staunchly loyal to the local shops. Frequenting the smaller spots paid off in many ways. One diary entry reads:

> *I went to the Wooten coffee shop and Princess Anne was at the next table. I saw her smiling at me and I smiled back but had only seen her at Johnny Bell-Irving's hunter-trials when she and her husband used to bring their horses to Dumfriesshire. Today the Princess had on a lavender mauve suit to match her car outside, a huge sports car; and I remembered my head scarf I was wearing was exactly the same color so I guessed that may have been why she smiled.*

Joannah's children were old enough to travel independently by the late 1980s, and they often made their way to Dursley for visits. Felicity's diary reflects the pride and concern she felt for her grandchildren. When a grandson graduated from university and began working in China just prior to the Tiananmen Square protests, Felicity wrote:

> *No word from Alexander in China. The unrest began with May Day when he was taking 100 children to Mao's grave in one railway coach. As I read this my heart sank and then the news broke that the protesting students were later just gunned down. It seems that the government has slipped back into the old ways of the emperors and no chance for the people to make their will felt or voices heard.*

Felicity was always far more concerned for people than politics. A few days later, she reported that Alexander had safely returned to the United States. Diary entries about time spent in Felicity's company are just as indicative of her verve for life. One granddaughter brought her own child to visit the Dursley cottage a decade later. The little girl* delighted in petting Felicity's rabbit, wandering through the garden, and watching her great-grandmother sketch.

Visits from family members living in the United States were treasured, but equally important were interactions with those still living in England. Miranda's son Jack developed a strong bond with his grandmother. Watching his swimming lessons at the Dursley indoor pool or supporting his studies at the Mary Katherine Lady Berkeley School in Kingswood were often highlights of Felicity's week. Jack kept in close contact with his grandmother while studying at Exeter University and pursuing graduate coursework in economics in preparation for an academic career.

Then there were Felicity's many friends and extended relatives who stopped by to admire her garden or enjoy tea. Rupert's nephew Marcus and his family often visited Felicity's Dursley home to play badminton or enjoy the animal-filled yard. Her godson Barty often popped in with his wife and son. He fondly recalls:

> *There were frequently visits, as we sat in the sunny living room, from birds through the open windows. I saw a robin*

and a blackbird come to a plate for crumbs, but once she was alone I believe some shyer ones would perch on her. Felicity had the artist's ability to sit still observing and to find nature where she was, without having to go to find it: not just the birds but hedgehogs, mice and butterflies settled around her as she worked intently on her weaving or drawing, quietly in the garden.

Neils Bolwig, a Danish zoologist, and his English wife Ingrid met Piers in Oklahoma, and to their mutual pleasure found they had overlapping interests from their earlier years living in South Africa with their two daughters. By coincidence, they moved to Gloucestershire for retirement where they soon became friends with Felicity, especially when she found that Neils was interested in nature, as reflected in his book "From Mosquitoes to Elephants."

In the quiet moments when Felicity was not entertaining guests, she turned to weaving and knitting. The large commercial pieces that she wove in her early twenties upon returning from Italy were no longer practical projects. Instead, she used a tablet loom to weave colorful trims for knitwear produced on a knitting machine. Alternatively, her sweaters were embroidered with silk sent by her grandson from China and carefully affixed with an identifying label. Along with her fingerless work-gloves they were given as gifts or sold in America through Joannah. Recipients of Felicity's art, painted and knitted alike, always marveled at her originality.

---

[50] "History." *Frenchay Village Museum.* Web.
[51] Barton, Andrew. "Industry in Dursley." *Dursley Glos Web.* Web
* *Annah Otis, co-author.*

13
A Mole, a Wizard, a Scotsman

Among Felicity's favorite destinations alone or with company was Slimbridge, Britain's National Wildlife Wetland Centre. The property was founded in 1946 by Olympic sailor, World War II soldier, and renowned naturalist Sir Peter Scott. Lady Scott was a similarly devoted naturalist who could be seen walking the trails of the renowned habitat that she helped to create, and as a widow had continued to serve as an esteemed board member. Both Felicity and Rupert held a special place in their hearts for Sir Peter's books because of his inspiring life story and gift for portraying birds in their natural environments. Lady Scott was also well-liked, especially after she responded to one of Felicity's Christmas cards featuring an etched bird. The women exchanged holiday greetings for years afterward.

Felicity found inspiration for her paintings and drawings in the carefully preserved Slimbridge wetlands, which hosted dozens of species and an acclaimed conservation team. Her wonderfully animate renditions of wildfowl are not necessarily scientifically accurate, but Felicity thought that communications among bird

Top to bottom:

Heron, Flamingos, and Ducks on a Lake. Mixed media.
Duck Confronting a Goose. Mixed media.
Preening Flamingoes. Watercolor.

species was symbolic of world peace. She never relied on photographs and instead spent hours sketching from real life. The Slimbridge staff were often helpful in finding good subjects for Felicity's work. These newfound connections helped Jack land a temporary job with the Slimbridge maintenance team during a school break. He was perched on a ladder painting the new canteen when none other than the Queen of England and the Duke of Edinburgh, patrons of Slimbridge, stopped to make an introduction. For Felicity, Slimbridge remained a calming sanctuary away from the rush of everyday life.

Felidity observes birds in a Slimbridge blind, 1999.

Besides creating hundreds of paintings, drawings, and prints over the course of almost ten decades, Felicity also found time for writing. Her letters to friends and family number in the hundreds. These letters were, "reminiscent of her slightly quiet way of speaking which masked a sharp and enquiring mind," as a friend fondly mused years later. However, Felicity's paintings were always the primary focus. In a letter to Joannah, she wrote, "I've done a nice picture so now I must write a story to go with it."

"Your Truly Sincere Moley" was written for Annah*, her great granddaughter, and reflects Felicity's compassion for defenseless creatures adapting to habitat change. An excerpt from the story recounts Moley's experience when he confronts his new environment:

> *Because my name is Moley, I must explain why this is so. You must understand, firstly, that my Grannie was actually a Mole. She used to tell us about old times in her gentle voice, how she lived in Rangers wood and enjoyed the many wonderful smells, although she could never see it because all moles are blind. It could not prevent her from making beautiful tunnels and molehills made of finest soil that she had sieved with her toes and fingers as she tried to find enough to eat for herself and, later, her family. She would have to swallow sixty to seventy percent of her body weight in worms to keep alive. In wintertime she never drank anything, but in summer, she traveled a mile there and another back to find a stream.*

> *Higher up we looked back, and below lay our old haunts disguised as a lake. But not far now, and beckoning from a new burrow, should be my loving Grannie and Great Aunt Mole. Then had started the wettest autumn ever known in that part of England. The records proved it, and now the meadows were no longer shining pale green, and no human workers drove up and down preparing for spring. Water lay in long silvery stripes. I could see a crane enjoying it and black-headed gulls beginning to arrive with the copy-cat ducks following. It would not be long before the tides got higher and reached the muddy pools, which would start to taste a bit salty. Water rats swam among the tree roots and fiddler crabs began to make neat holes in the banks for my rabbit and mole relations to enlarge.*

It was all confusing to find our home becoming marshland. Then I saw my reflection in the huge puddles forming everywhere. In a flash, I knew the answer: I was a vole. The reddish tinge made my coat more attractive to look at than a rat. I was bigger than a mouse. I always wished to live near water.

Moley was inspired by Felicity's pet rabbit of the same name. The real-life Moley was a shy soul who never failed to make his mistress smile. It often took several introductions for him to feel comfortable with visitors. Another well-loved rabbit named Bunn may have been the inspiration for characters in other stories.

Pen and ink.

Even when Felicity's stories were told from the perspective of humans, they incorporated animal characters. "The Space Wizard" revolves around Paul and Pam and their neighborhood friends; and features an encounter with a wizard who grants Paul his wish to ride in a space ship with his two pets, the lobster Crusty and the spaniel Biddy. Although the story follows the classic model of books about children who experience their imaginary worlds first hand, Felicity up-dates these worlds and shows that she is in touch with children of her day.

Pam used to come home from school and find her triplet brothers turning everything upside down because their school finished early. She used to put on a sweater and a

> woolly cap if it was winter and go into the cul de sac to look for Paul and Fanny. On one particular day Fanny was sitting in the pram singing to herself very softly and playing with a pink rabbit. Paul was kicking a football about. As Fanny lifted the rabbit high above her head, it waived its whiskers and there was a peep noise. Paul and Pam looked up, and in the air above them there was a round friendly face of a wizard.
>
> The mouth was opening and they could see silver teeth inside. It spoke first to Paul who was dressed in pale blue jeans, and it said haughtily: "Your trousers are dirty," as Paul looked down at them, the wizard blew out its cheeks and puffed at the dirty marks till they disappeared. Then it asked, "What do you want to do most?" Paul thought, but Fanny dropped her rattle, so he had to go and pick it up. "Come on! Hurry up," said the wizard. Paul held himself straight and said, "Ride in a spaceship."

Felicity also dabbled in non-fiction writing. A lengthy history of the Graham family, which she spent many months researching at the local library and carefully composing on her manual typewriter, is one example. The first chapter offers an overview of her ancestors and a taste of her writing style:

> To understand people, we must know their background, and what brought them to their present state. Of their reputation, they can be so very proud. Everywhere in the English world, Scotsmen are respected; they are tough, but not rough, and they seem to possess imagination as well as stamina and courage. Their appalling climate has never daunted them. Possibly it fosters heroism. It was to the North the first saints came but woven into their history is much sadness. Their songs are mostly sad and haunting until we come to Harry Lauder, and the present-day image of the funny Scott in a kilt is a puerile one. Not so, the one of the ferocious Highlanders who lived up to their reputation

in World Wars One and Two. Lowlanders are a different breed; they must be extremely resilient to survive all the awfulness of their past. For generations, they seem to have lived in a no-man's land where different companies of warriors surged back and forth at their master's will in order to subject and frighten, kill, rape, and murder the inhabitants for sport or vengeance. No comfortable manor houses were left standing here; every building has been burned down many times and rebuilt. The cottages are of the simplest pattern because the owners knew them to be impermanent. Only ideas were permanent; the feuds lasted for generations.

Captain William Fergus Graham OBE with his Terriers at Mossknowe near Kirkpatrick Fleming, c. 1950. Major Claude Graham's (p. 84) oldest brother and head of the Grahm household.

The Graham dwelling was a fortified tower north of Carlisle, and no longer exists. A Graham married an Irving and some of her stone house still stands; the present house only dates from the middle of the 18th century. Built by a Graham *come home from the West Indies, he employed a Mr. Craig or Craik from Arbigland on the other side of the Solway. He is mentioned in the history of Dumfries, but not as an architect. He used the soft pink sandstone from nearby quarries, and the marble in the sitting room mantelpiece is from Cumbria. The house is not typically early Georgian, but has a strong colonial flavor imparted by the sugar-growing Dr. William who made enough money with his sugar to buy in Mossknowe estate, which had been sold by William Graham and Isabella (née Herries) after 13 children had been born to them. The estate had been sequestered and exposed to roup. Dr. William succeeded Fergus who had been exiled after the 1715 rebellion, and a politically active Fergus lived in semi-hiding at Mossknowe. Unfortunately, he quarreled with one Scott about a girl, and slew him, so we will hope this was a case of rough justice. When Dr. William rebuilt the house, the master mason was very appropriately Simon Porteous. William had been living at Bluefields in Jamaica, and the massive piece of Spanish mahogany he managed to bring home is now the dining-room table.*

Barely in Scotland, Mossknowe is the home of a Scottish family, until my mother's generation they proudly married into other Scottish families.

These excerpts offer a lasting record of Felicity's direct, yet kind, approach to life.

Pen and ink.

Felicity enjoys the view from her room at the Steppes in Nailworth, 2009.

14

THE WANING YEARS

On the first day of May in 1992, Rupert suddenly died of a heart attack at age eighty-one. He was scheduled to visit Felicity that week, but travel plans had to make way for funeral preparations. Rupert was buried in the family cemetery at Matfen Hall following a well-attended service marked by kind words and fond memories. Though the Blacketts had been separated for ten years, Rupert's death was a great loss to Felicity.

Felicity bore her grief gracefully, perhaps because life had forced her to learn how to cope with loss. At age eighty, she substituted her car for a three-speed bicycle outfitted with a basket for carrying groceries. The hilly one-mile road to Dursley regularly saw her sprightly form pedaling to and fro. Much of Felicity's time was occupied by taking care of her animals or painting canvases to be sold in a Nailsworth gallery. However, she reserved several hours per week for teaching art classes at the Fernie Hill Rehabilitation Center. It was only in her ninetieth year that age and aches began to catch up.

To mark Felicity's ninetieth birthday in 2002, family members from around the world gathered at Slimbridge. Her nephew Marcus attended with his wife Chia-Li and their first child, Charles. The couple met while they were both teaching in a Rudolf Steiner school and later moved near-by to Stroud. Several years after the celebration, they welcomed a baby girl named Eily. Marcus's sister Polly made the trip from London where she had a career in art restoration. The Blackett siblings occasionally called on Piers in Oklahoma and Joannah in New Jersey en route to see their mother's family in Chile. Jack was well on his way to becoming a Lecturer in Economics by this point, but he and Miranda set aside the day to celebrate. Piers took some time off from the Oklahoma City hospital to join them.

The Wilmerding half of Felicity's ninetieth party crossed the Atlantic to celebrate as well. Joannah and Harry traveled to England as frequently as busy schedules allowed. Their daughter Felicity, who worked as an art appraiser in New Jersey, accompanied them with her daughter Annah. Alexander Wilmerding, Felicity's older brother, attended the party with his wife Ginny and their son Nicholas. The couple enjoyed successful business careers in Boston and Hong Kong, where they raised Nicholas as well as a younger daughter named Mimi.

A bout of pneumonia followed by a long recovery period in the Berkeley Hospital, one of England's few remaining cottage hospitals, necessitated new living arrangements. Felicity dreaded the prospect of living alone with an aide, so she urged Joannah and Miranda to find her an elderly community where she might enjoy the company of others. The Steppes Residential Care Home in Nailsworth was deemed the best option since it gave Felicity access to the shops and parks of a fairly active village while providing medical support. Her room afforded views of a stream running through the garden. The home's tool shed soon became her personal insect habitat. Staff quickly learned to avoid cleaning the caterpillar hatchery resting on her window sill.

Double hip replacement and cataract removal surgery posed minor stumbling blocks in the last ten years of Felicity's life. With each operation, the therapeutic nature of painting became all the more important. Egg tempera which Piers sent his mother from America became her medium of choice. The paint is opaque and handles like oils although it is water based and leaves a chalky finish. Three of her still lifes done in this medium remain hanging in The Steppes Care Home to this day. These later canvases tend towards the abstract; flowers and bugs manifest as undulating forms.

Miranda continued to take her mother on much-cherished trips to nearby National Trust properties for artistic inspiration. Felicity's godson Barty was a faithful and entertaining visitor and Hilary, a family friend from South Africa, brought her husband. Felicity's cousin Susannah drove from Kent to spend the afternoon, and a neighbor in Dursley brought her flowers from the garden on her motorcycle. Felicity also found companionship in her massage therapist, Mikiko Cameron, who remained a devoted friend until the last.

Even as her strength and stamina failed, Felicity maintained a remarkably sharp sense of humor and awareness. Being wheelchair-bound never took the joy out of going to a local health food store called the Green Spirit for a cup of coffee or a glass of elderflower cordial. In her dwindling years, Felicity occasionally looked back over the course of her life.

A poem titled "The Loom of Time," translated from Kalidasa, the 5th century greatest sanskrit poet, which she had carefully copied in pen-and-ink, was found in her bedside drawer. An excerpt reads:

> *Not 'til the loom is silent*
> *When the shuttles cease to fly,*
> *Shall God reveal the pattern*
> *That explains the reasons why...*

Death was not necessarily something Felicity feared. She once mused, "It is always a sad puzzle not knowing where we shall be going after this planet" and advised family "to keep in touch with everyone possible" as she neared the end. A Catholic priest named Father Rainbow performed last rites, which was an uplifting and deeply spiritual moment for Felicity. She passed peacefully in her sleep at the wizened age of ninety-nine. Friends and family gathered to say their goodbyes at a Catholic funeral service near Dursley before transferring her ashes to their final resting place beside Rupert in the Holy Trinity Churchyard near Matfen Hall.

A poet Felicity came to love in her later years, William Cowper, wrote a few verses with great resonance to Felicity's remarkable life:

> *Here, sweetly forgetting and wholly forgot*
> *By the world and its turbulent throng*
> *The birds and the streams lend me many a note*
> *That aids meditation and song.*

Her ninety-nine years were marked by war, peace, and painting. They will be fondly remembered.

Remembering Felicity

Felicity touched so many lives during her yeas in England, Italy, Germany and South Africa. Reflections and fond memories from those who knew her best have been compiled here.

Felicity Wilmerding, *Felicity Blackett's grand-daughter*

Grannie's regime was exemplary as she maintained a full schedule bicycling, gardening, painting, knitting and walking. When visiting Grannie, one realized how well-disciplined she was as we would try to keep up with and participate in her activities, whether walking the hillside paths behind the house to see the view of the River Severn, collecting dandelions up the lane for Bun-Bun, pedaling to town, or pushing the bladed mower.

Linda Duncan, *Felicity's friend from Oklahoma*

Felicity Blackett was unforgettable. Peter and I thought she was quite an amazing lady when we first met her in her cottage where she had ducks. At that time she was riding her bicycle into town and selling her duck eggs.

Our next two visits were to The Steppes. During that time Felicity taught us about her insect friends and the birds who visited her regularly.

Our last memory is driving away from The Steppes... Felicity elegantly saluted us with her left cane and then her right cane. Felicity was loved and admired by all that knew her. She was so kind and a great correspondent and artist. I still have one of her hand drawn and colored Christmas cards.

Barty Wordsworth, *Felicity's godson*

At Dursley, her ducks included domesticated mallards and farmyard whites. Then gradually over time they were all Indian Runners. Why? I asked once. After getting a single one, she had learnt that their intelligence was greater, or at least they were more attuned to her. Also, because they are lean and tall, perhaps they were even more physically alike? Anyway, they also took more care of her plants, were less clumsy when feeding and left less collateral damage, less breakage of stems, less damage to the grass.

At The Steppes, Felicity had a jar of miscellaneous grasses and vegetation which was in fact a vivarium for caterpillars, a hatchery for moths and even butterflies. The staff quickly learned not to try to tidy away and clean her vivarium! Even finally once she was more or less bedbound, she was able to maintain her awareness of the birds that visited the trees within view of her window.

Hilary Butler, née Arderne,
Felicity's family friend from her time in South Africa

Felicity, Rupert and their family were a major feature of our lives in the Cape. My parents had met them when abroad with the Durham Light Infantry, and when the Blacketts decided to move to South Africa, their friendship was cemented.

My husband and I visited Felicity twice in England. The first time was at Dursley in her lovely little home outside the village. We spent quite a bit of time in her garden amongst the ducks and rabbits, learning about their habits. Once inside the house, we were surprised to see a lovely bunny eating the edge of her Persian carpet; when we pointed out the problem, Felicity calmly said, "Oh, she loves that carpet!" We also visited her at The Steppes shortly before she died. She was walking with two canes and had slowed down considerably; however, her room, with a lovely view over the garden, was alive with plants in various containers and lots of canvases and paints. She was the same as ever, very pleased to see us and full of questions about our life and family in Canada.

We never called Felicity "Aunt" as with our parents' other friends. She was just too young, right until the end of her life.

Jo Smith, *Manager of The Steppes, Nailsworth, Gloucestershire.*

We still have Felicity's paintings up on our walls and people comment how lovely they are. I am always very proud to say Felicity lived here at The Steppes with us.

Felicity was a very unique lady, never before or since have I met anyone quite like her. She was a softly spoken, warm hearted, strong, talented, inspirational gem.

Emma remembers Felicity and we have been reminiscing. The skin cancer she cured on her leg with leaves and manuka honey, Dr Booker couldn't believe it. Her wonderful smile. The smell of the egg tempura paint in her room. Her love of nature, the bee she tried to bring back to life even though it was slightly mummified. She gave us some great memories.

Felicity's Family

A tree drawn to clarify relationship

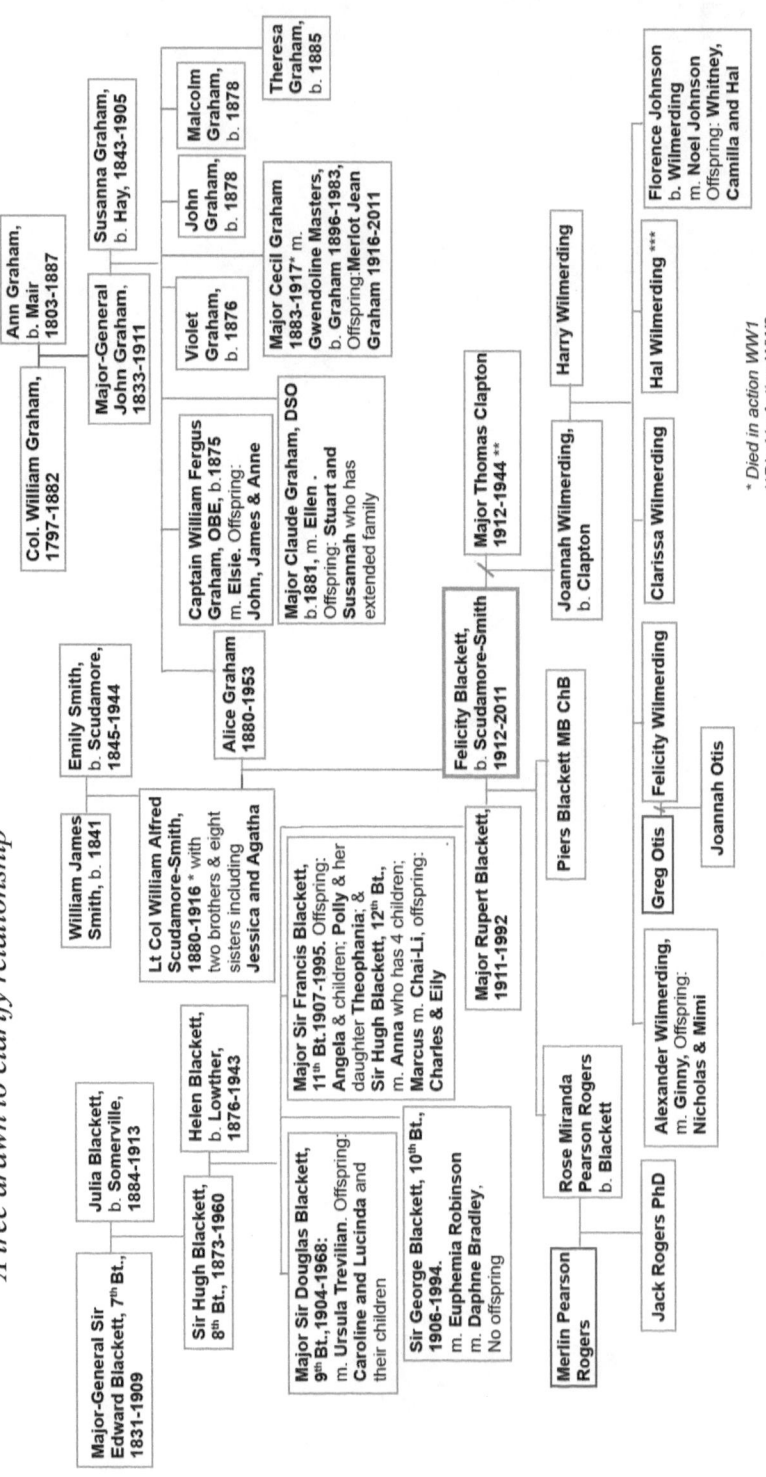

Selected Bibliography

Altman, Lawrence. "Christiaan Barnard, 78, Surgeon for First Heart Transplant, Dies." *New York Times,* September 3, 2001, Web.

Barton, Andrew. "Industry in Dursley." *Dursley Glos Web.* Web. <http://www.dursleyglos.org.uk/html/dursley/industry/industry.htm>.

Burke, Bernard. *A Genealogical and Heraldic History of the Landed Gentry of Great Britain & Ireland.* 9th ed. London, UK: Harrison & Sons, 1898. Print.

"Castle." *Hampton Court Castle.* Web. <https://www.hamptoncourtcastle.co.uk/castle>.

"Charles Pratt & Company, LLC." Web. <http://www.charlespratt.com/index2.html>.

Churchill, Winston S. *The World Crisis, 1911-1918.* London, UK: T. Butterworth, 1931. Print.

Davidson, W. E. Peace *Treaty of Vereeniging.* Tran. Government of South African Republic and the British Government., 1902. Print.

Dunnage, Jonathan. *Twentieth Century Italy:* A Social History. New York, NY: Routledge, 2014. Print.

Farrer, William, and J. Brownbill. "Townships: Knowsley." *A History of the County of Lancaster: Volume 3.* London, UK: Victoria County History, 1907. 157-168. Print.

"Frenchay Hospital Prepares to Take its Place in History." *Western Daily Press,* January 28, 2014, Web. <https://web.archive.org/web/20140530001216/http://www.westerndailypress.co.uk/Frenchay-Hospital-prepares-place-history/story-20509970-detail/story.html>.

"George." *South African History Online.* March 2011. Web. <https://www.sahistory.org.za/place/george>.

Green, Lawrence G. *South African Beachcomber.* Cape Town, ZA: Timmins, 1964. Print.

"Hereford Journal." *Hereford Journal,* April 18, 1903, p. 5. Web.

"History." *Frenchay Village Museum.* a. Web. <https://www.frenchaymuseumarchives.co.uk/MuseumPage04-History.htm>.

"History." *The Hereford Cattle Society.* b. Web. <http://www.herefordcattle.org/about-us/history/>.

Johnson, Nelson. *Battleground New Jersey: Vanderbilt, Hague, and their Fight for Justice.* New Brunswick, NJ: Rutgers University Press, 2014. Print.

Kershaw, Roger. "Remembering the City of Benares Tragedy." *The National Archives.* September 17, 2015. Web. <https://blog.nationalarchives.gov.uk/remembering-city-benares-tragedy/>.

Kirtley, Allan, Patricia Longbottom, and Martin Blackett. *A History of the Blacketts: The Story of a Remarkable North-East England Family Over Seven Centuries.* UK: The Blacketts, 2013. Print.

"Kruger National Park." *South African National Parks.* Web. <http://www.sanparks.org/parks/kruger/default.php/>.

Kuznets, Lois R. *Kenneth Grahame.* Boston, MA: Twayne Publishers, 1987. Print.

Laws, David. *Who Killed Kitchener? the Life and Death of Britain's most Famous War Minister.* London, UK: Biteback Publishing, 2020. Print.

Selected Bibliography

"Leominster Agricultural Society's Show." *Wellington Journal and Shrewsbury News,* September 10, 1887, p. 3. Web.

Limb, Peter. *African National Congress.* Lynne Rienner Publishers, Inc., 2011. Web.

Liverpool City Council. *The Merseyside Historic Characterisation Project: Liverpool.* Liverpool, UK: National Museums Liverpool, 2009. Print.

Lord, Walter. *A Night to Remember: The Classic Account of the Final Hours of the Titanic.* New York, NY: Griffin, 2005. Print.

Lukacs, John R. *Blood, Toil, Tears and Sweat: The Dire Warning: Churchill's First Speech as Prime Minister.* New York, NY: Basic Books 2008. Print.

MacMillan, Harold. *The Wind of Change.* Tran. South African Parliament. Print.

Maddocks, Graham. *Liverpool Pals: A History of the 17th, 18th, 19th and 20th Service Service Battalions, the King's Liverpool Regiment 1914-1919.* London, UK: Leo Cooper, 1991. Print.

"Mass Observation, 1937-1950s." Mass Observation. <http://www.massobs.org.uk/mass-observation-1937-1950s>.

Meredith, Martin. *Diamonds, Gold, and War: The British, the Boers, and the Making of South Africa.* New York, NY: Public Affairs, 2008. Print.

Muir, Ramsay. *A History of Liverpool.* 2nd ed. London, UK: University Press of Liverpool, 1907. Print.

Myers, Frank. "Harold Macmillan's "Winds of Change" Speech: A Case Study in the Rhetoric of Policy Change." *Rhetoric and Public Affairs* 3.4 (2000): 555-75. Web.

Norris, C. N. F. "Obituary: Lord Cheshire VC." *The Independent,* August 1, 1992, Web.

Oddy, Derek J. "The Stop-Go Era: Restoring Food Choice in Britain After World War II." *The Rise of Obesity in Europe: A Twentieth Century Food History.* Surrey, UK: Ashgate Publishing Ltd., 2009. 59-76. Print.

"Our History." *Wildfowl & Wetlands Trust.* Web. <https://www.wwt.org.uk/who-we-are/our-history>.

Poole, David. "Dinmore Manor House." *House and Heritage.* May 2, 2018. Web. <https://houseandheritage.org/2018/05/02/dinmore-manor-house/>.

"Richard Annand." *The English Light Infantry.* Web. <http://www.lightinfantry.me.uk/vcrannand.htm>.

Rissik, David. D.L.I. *AT WAR: The History of the Durham Light Infantry 1939-1945.* Naval & Military Press, 2004. Print.

Robinson, Bruce. *"The Pals Batallions in World War One." BBC.* 2011. Web. <http://www.bbc.co.uk/history/british/britain_wwone/pals_01.shtml>.

The Scottish Antiquary, Or Northern Notes and Queries. Ed. A. W. Hallen. Edinburgh, Scotland: Constable, T. & A., 1894. Print.

Sharpeville Massacre. Eds. K. Johnson and S. Jacobs. Boulder, CO: Lynne Rienner Publishers, Inc., 2011. Print.

Sheffield, Gary. "The Origins of World War One." BBC. March 2011. Web. <http://www.bbc.co.uk/history/worldwars/wwone/origins_01.shtml>.

Simkins, Peter. *Kitchener's Army: The Raising of the New Armies 1914-1916.* Philadelphia, PA: Casemate Publishers, 2007. Print.

"Situating India." *India: Emerging Power.* Washington, DC: Brookings Institution Press, 2001. 7-35. Print.

Thompson, Leonard. *A History of South Africa.* 3rd ed. New Haven, CT: Yale University Press, 2001. Print.

Waddy, Nicholas L. "The Fork in the Road? British Reactions to the Election of an Apartheid Government in South Africa, may 1948." *Historia* 55.1 (2010)Web.

Wasson, Ellis. *A History of Modern Britain: 1714 to the Present.* 2nd ed. West Sussex, UK: John Wiley & Sons, Inc, 2016. Print.

Welshman, John. *Churchill's Children: The Evacuee Experience in Wartime Britain.* Oxford, UK: Oxford University Press, 2010. Print.

Selected Bibliography

Wessels, Andries. "An Irish Gentleman in Africa: The Ambiguous Political and Cultural Identity of Sir Percy FitzPatrick." *English in Africa* 31.1 (2004): 5-22. Print.

Westlake, Ray. *Tracing British Battalions on the Somme.* Barnsley, UK: Pen and Sword Military, 2009. Print.

Wilfrith, Elstob. *Sixteenth, Seventeenth, Eighteenth & Nineteenth Battalions: The Manchester Regiment 1914-1918.* Naval and Military Press, 2009. *Print.*

www.ingramcontent.com/pod-product-compliance
Lightning Source LLC
LaVergne TN
LVHW092051060526
838201LV00047B/1336